Praise for *Reinventing the Leader*

"*Reinventing the Leader* is an inspiring account of the magic that can happen when a leader realizes they must undergo their own transformation in order to transform their organization. Entertaining and relevant, the book includes personal insights from both authors while showing the pivotal role that trust plays in the leader/coach relationship. Gui Loureiro and Carlos Marin have written an honest, vulnerable, and praiseworthy book that should be in the library of every leader and coach."

—Ken Blanchard, coauthor, *The One Minute Manager®* and *Simple Truths of Leadership*

"In his account of the digital transformation of Walmart Mexico and Central America (Walmex), Gui Loureiro has provided a textbook on leading through change. He not only reinvented the business while also delivering results, but he also reinvented himself as a new kind of leader. The only constant in retail today is change, and Gui adopted a change mindset, which, combined with his commitment to our purpose and values, helped propel Walmex to being one of the most customer-centric parts of our company.

What I love most about this story is how Gui, with the support of his executive coach Carlos Marin, flipped his view to start from the inside out. He started by changing himself, his mindset and approach, which resulted in a positive outcome for the people around him and our business. This isn't easy to do. It's so much easier to talk about change with others than it is to change ourselves.

Gui tells the Walmex story with the honesty, vulnerability and humanity that lend him a truly authentic voice. You can't help but like this guy. And you won't finish this book without sharing my enormous respect for what he accomplished – and how."

—Doug McMillon, President and CEO, Walmart

"You'll find no business jargon or easy aha moments in this remarkable book. Rather, it offers the at-times painfully honest story of a highly visible CEO with sufficient humility to realize that *he* needed to change before he could transform his company. It also shows how the relationship between a coach and coachee can spur growth, insight, and trust. Written with welcome clarity, this business narrative grabs you from the first page. Highly recommended for leaders and for coaches."

—Sally Helgesen, Author, *How Women Rise, Rising Together,* and *The Female Advantage*

"*Reinventing the Leader* is among the most compelling business leadership books I've read in a long time. It's exceedingly rare when both the dynamic CEO of a huge, iconic retail business and his seasoned executive coach tell all—in their own unvarnished words, and in the words of executives around them—about the dreams and fears they shared before, during, and after a major transformation of the business, which had to succeed and from which there was no turning back. In addition to recounting the fascinating story of their journey of learning and changing together, Gui Loureiro and Carlos Marin populate each chapter with hands-on tips and techniques that executives orchestrating change in their own organizations can use. In these turbulent times, I can't imagine more relevant reading for all current and aspiring leaders!"

—John Alexander, President, Leadership Horizons, and former
President and CEO, Center for Creative Leadership

"*Reinventing the Leader* is built on the rich experiences and remarkable introspections from two exceptional global business and thought leaders. At a time when change is omnipresent, this book offers very valuable guidance on successfully inspiring, delivering and communicating optimal change and leadership. More importantly, it provides unique insights on how to lead change by transforming yourself to better serve all your stakeholders. It is truly one of the most inspiring leadership books I have read over the last 10 years, and I recommend it to anyone who wants to drive change and reinvent themselves for greater impact."

—Dr. Dominique Turpin, Emeritus Professor and former Dean and President,
IMD, European President of CEIBS, Chairman of DAA Capital

"*Reinventing the Leader* is a master class in leader growth and learning. It's a unique, behind-the-scenes look into one leader's efforts to transform a business and a coach's reflections on leader reinvention. With vulnerability, humility, and transparency, Gui Loureiro and Carlos Marin reveal workplace change through two distinct perspectives—the leader's and the coach's—enabling the reader to appreciate how the leader-coach partnership works. In the process, we see how changing organizations also means changing oneself. *Reinventing the Leader* should be required reading for every leader and student of leadership."

—Jim Kouzes, Bestselling Coauthor, *The Leadership Challenge*, and
a Fellow, Doerr Institute for New Leaders, Rice University

"*Reinventing the Leader* is a groundbreaking and insightful guide for leaders looking to effect meaningful change within their organizations. Gui Loureiro and Carlos E. Marin masterfully argue that the key to transforming a company begins with the transformation of the leader themselves. With practical tools, compelling case studies, and a deep understanding of the evolving challenges in today's business world, this book offers a roadmap for personal and professional growth that is essential for leading successful, innovative teams. By shifting the focus to self-awareness, adaptive thinking, and emotional intelligence, Loureiro and Marin provide a powerful framework for leaders to inspire real change. This is a must-read for anyone looking to lead with purpose and impact in an increasingly complex business landscape."

—C.J. Fitzgerald, 25-Year Private Equity Veteran

Reinventing the Leader

Reinventing the Leader

How to Change Yourself to Change Your Company

Guilherme Loureiro and Carlos E. Marin

Matt Holt Books
An Imprint of BenBella Books, Inc.
Dallas, TX

Matt Holt is an imprint of BenBella Books, Inc.
8080 N. Central Expressway
Suite 1700
Dallas, TX 75206
benbellabooks.com
Send feedback to feedback@benbellabooks.com

BenBella and *Matt Holt* are federally registered trademarks.

Printed in the United States of America
10 9 8 7 6 5 4 3 2 1

Library of Congress Control Number: 2024052048
ISBN 978-1-63774-680-6 (hardcover)
ISBN 978-1-63774-681-3 (electronic)

Editing by Katie Dickman
Copyediting by Michael Fedison
Proofreading by Cheryl Beacham and Marissa Wold Uhrina
Text design and composition by Aaron Edmiston
Cover design by Raul Loureiro
Printed by Lake Book Manufacturing

From Guilherme:

To my parents, Flavio and Zuleida—you gave me the values, the example, and the love. For that, I am forever grateful. You opened up new worlds of possibility for me and taught me to love learning.

To my wife, Patricia—you are the one who encouraged me to change and made me feel I was never alone in my journey of reinvention. It was you I turned to for support when I made mistakes, and it was you who helped me celebrate each improvement (even the smallest ones that took others time to see). Change is challenging and you were my safe harbor when the seas became rough. Thank you for the laughter and the long debates too. Your steadfast support over the years gave me strength, and my success was possible because you were always by my side.

To my kids, Pedro, Dado, and Fei—you are everything to me and it is because of your love that I wanted to be better than I was, to live up to your respect. This book is my legacy to you.

From Carlos:

To my dear wife, Martha, my partner in life's journey, your love and support are my anchor. Your unshakable spiritual faith is a source of inspiration.

To my son, Carlos Jr., my pride and joy. You have filled my world with wonder and purpose. You became one of my teachers the moment you came into our world.

To my cherished grandchildren, Lucas and Naila, you are the stars that light up my sky. Your laughter echoes through the halls of my heart, and your innocence reminds me of life's simple joys. May you grow, explore, and find magic in every moment.

To my beloved parents, Hernan Marin and Clara Portilla de Marin, I will forever be in gratitude for your unwavering love, guidance, and sacrifices that allowed me to pursue my dreams.

To the leaders and change-makers of today and tomorrow, who have the courage, vision, and passion to transform themselves and their organizations for the better. This book is dedicated to you and your noble endeavors. May you find inspiration, guidance, and wisdom in these pages.

Author's Note from Gui

During the final stages of working on *Reinventing the Leader* my role expanded from CEO of Walmex (Walmart Mexico and Central America) to Chairman of the Board for Walmex and Regional CEO for Canada, Chile, Central America, and Mexico. The added countries will mean added responsibilities; however, since *Reinventing the Leader* is specifically about the transformation of Walmex, we have chosen to refer only to my title at that time throughout the book.

Contents

Foreword

by Dr. Marshall Goldsmith

In *Reinventing the Leader,* Guilherme Loureiro and Carlos Marin offer an essential and powerful Guide for modern leadership. Drawing on Guilherme's wisdom as a seasoned CEO, including his transformative time as CEO at Walmart Mexico and Central America, and Carlos's extensive background in leadership development and as an international executive, they present a narrative that is as much about personal growth as it is about guiding others. Their book is not just a reflection, but a call to action for leaders to evolve with vision and integrity in an era marked by profound change.

Reinventing the Leader arrives at a pivotal moment for current and aspiring leaders who face the dual challenges of rapid technological change and the evolving needs of their teams. This book is a call for leaders to embrace the mindset of continuous learning and growth. It offers a unique value proposition by blending the conceptual frameworks of leadership with practical, actionable insights drawn from the rich experiences of its authors. The dynamic combination of Guilherme's digital transformation expertise and Carlos's leadership coaching acumen provides a rare, dual perspective that is deeply needed in the literature of leadership development.

They also emphasize the collective journey of leadership—how it thrives on strong, diverse teams and inclusive cultures. They argue that true leadership empowers others, creating an environment where each member can contribute to their fullest potential. This collaborative approach is central to the adaptability and success of modern organizations, as demonstrated by Guilherme's and Carlos's respective professional achievements.

As an experienced mentor to global leaders, I've seen the transformative influence of leaders who embody these principles. Guilherme and Carlos offer a dynamic perspective on leadership that is critical for today's technology-dependent organizations. This book is a treasure chest of wisdom for impactful leadership, offering the mindset and the means to truly make a difference. It is a guide for aspiring leaders to not just succeed, but to lead purposefully and leave a lasting legacy.

Reinventing the Leader emerges as a testament to the power of leadership transformation—one that's deeply needed in our business world. Guilherme and Carlos offer their storied achievements not just as a backdrop, but as living proof that the principles they share are time-tested and effective. This book is poised to become an essential instrument for any leader looking to make an indelible mark in their organization and beyond.

Dr. Marshall Goldsmith is the *Thinkers50* World's #1 Executive Coach and *New York Times* best-selling author of *The Earned Life*, *Triggers*, and *What Got You Here Won't Get You There*.

The Drivers and Challenges of Change

"You cannot swim for new horizons until you have
courage to lose sight of the shore."
—William Faulkner

The Call, March 2018

Gui

"I need your help." Those were the first words I said to my friend Carlos Marin, one of the foremost executive coaches to top business leaders all over the world. It was a call I never thought I'd have to make under these circumstances.

As the new CEO of Walmex, a division of Walmart and Mexico's biggest retailer, I had been tasked with convincing the company that despite their years of success, they needed to dramatically change in order to excel in the future. A tall order, for sure, but I had looked at it as an exciting opportunity—a challenge—and believed I was the leader who could meet the moment and bring a trusted chain of brick-and-mortar stores into the digital economy. In my first year I received an excellent performance review from my boss, but after a successful second year at the helm I was met with a critical annual appraisal. I suddenly wondered, *Am I the leader for the job at* this *company?*

At the end of December 2017, right before I flew back to Brazil to spend time with my family, I met with my boss to review the past year—my second as CEO of Walmex. Under previous leadership, the company had experienced a couple of years of results below expectations (a rare situation for Walmex), but during the year before my arrival and my first year we were in top form again, delivering great results, and the overall feeling was that "we were back."

While everybody else was celebrating what we had accomplished and the bonuses they had earned, I started thinking about the future. I still only had a hazy idea at that time about how we would change, but the one thing that was crystal clear to me was that in order to maintain our edge, we needed to reinvent ourselves, leveraging technology to compete in the world of e-commerce. We had begun the early stages of the transformation process and we were already starting to see promising advances in our shift to a multidisciplinary model with a focus on digital operations.

I was close to my boss, and as he entered my office, I expected a quick, even celebratory, meeting.

He started out by saying, "Congratulations on another great year. There is nothing I can say other than well done—and thank you. The results speak to your excellent leadership."

"Thank you."

There was a pause, and I could tell my boss was carefully choosing his words. "However, there is one thing I want to discuss with you that is worrying me a lot."

"Please, tell me."

He looked me straight in the eyes as he spoke, as if to gauge the effect of what he was about to tell me. "It seems that your style is scaring people. We also have feedback that your passion leads you to act in emotional ways that can have a negative impact on those around you. It's reaching a point where you'll need to change and do it fast."

"I don't know what you're talking about," I said, shocked at what I was hearing. "I'm close to our associates, have good communication with them, and I've never had a problem like this in my life. Where does it come from?" Before my boss could even respond, I added, "Let's take a walk around the office and you'll see how people approach me, how they talk with me, and it will prove to you that I don't 'scare' them."

My boss leaned toward me. "Gui, you need to take this very seriously. This is a big problem, and you need to work on it. Talk to your HR partner about helping you."

I felt like a bomb had gone off in my head. I told my boss, "I spend a whole year working hard and now you and my HR 'partner' come up with this surprise?"

I refused to sign my appraisal because in my mind it described someone with bad intentions, and I did not see myself as that person. I was not thinking clearly, and I became convinced that for some unknown reason someone wanted to cause damage to my career.

After the meeting, I couldn't relax. I was furious and felt betrayed by my boss and my HR partner. This was the first time my behavior had ever been questioned at an appraisal. I had always received feedback that I was a very caring human being. What had changed now—*and why?*

After flying back to Brazil, I received a phone call the next day from my boss. He offered to tone down the appraisal, adding, "But I'm asking you to see this feedback as serious and constructive."

Several heated conversations followed, and I suggested to my boss that we should hire a coach to work with me and help me further understand what the issues were. I was familiar with Carlos because he was already doing a superb job coaching my executive committee to prepare them for the transformation. In addition, when I was CEO at Unilever Mexico, he had been immensely helpful to me, conducting a team integration workshop with my national executive committee to help us redefine our strategic priorities and identify key behaviors to help us work collaboratively. There was no one I trusted more to be my coach, so I suggested to my boss that Carlos could work personally with me as well as continue coaching my team.

Finally, in March 2018, my boss gave me the green light and I immediately called Carlos and asked him to become my coach at Walmex. I secretly hoped that he would talk to people on my team and discover that some kind of widespread issue simply did not exist, that it was only an isolated case of somebody making a complaint and my boss turning it into a larger problem than it really was.

"Tell me what's going on," requested Carlos.

"I received a bad appraisal from my boss—and that was after a terrific second year. We agreed to hire you as my coach to help us get to the bottom of what the issue is since the two of us cannot agree."

"I want to be of help," said Carlos. "And it would be a pleasure to work with you again."

"You know me, Carlos. You know how deeply I care about my associates and that I'm passionate about my work. *Can you believe that my boss told me that I'm scaring people?* I feel like he's telling me that I'm not treating them well and that's simply not true! If I'm truly the person described in this evaluation, I cannot be the CEO of this company."

Luckily, Carlos always stays on an even keel, even when I don't. He said, "Gui, you know how much I appreciate working with you—but you'll need to calm down and listen. You must try not to take what your boss said too personally."

"Okay," I said, "but this is serious—and I need you to help me get to the truth."

Carlos asked, "Will you allow me to talk openly and listen to your team to fully understand the issue?"

"Yes, of course," I replied. "You know how much I trust you. And nothing is more important than figuring out what's going on."

Gui

Reinventing the Leader is a chronicle of monumental change, both in myself and within the company I lead, for I believe a leader must grow to achieve sustainable growth in the organization. This book is a blueprint for transformational success for leaders in any business who find themselves facing the need to retool their own company's systems and operations and energize and inspire an entire corporate culture in order to compete in an ever-shifting digital economy. It's about sustaining a cherished brand while disrupting the very essence of how it's done business in the past. And perhaps most important of all, it's about *learning to learn*—becoming aware of how to better leverage your strengths, limit your weaknesses, and listen more effectively to your associates and customers to find out what they really want and *need* during a time of major transition.

In this journey of transformation, we will reflect on how I reinvented myself in order to effectively change the company. Carlos and I will endeavor to provide you with a training manual for leaders, to candidly reveal from our two perspectives the essential truths we learned as we traveled a path that was sometimes rocky, sometimes uncertain, and ultimately rewarding, both personally and professionally.

This is the story of how we succeeded in our mission by allowing ourselves and the organization to be guided by Sam Walton's original purpose for creating Walmart back in 1962. The resurgent power of his vision defined why we were driven to be so committed to this unprecedented transformation. We were inspired by his strong sense of purpose to save people money so they could live better lives, at every step respecting all individuals and striving for excellence with integrity. In this age of e-commerce, we employed the tools of technology to empower our customers to shop online; using agile methodology and data analytics, we began to think of innovative ways to help them.

With *Reinventing the Leader*, our goal is to energize you to find the purpose that is bigger than yourself or the company, that transcends a computer screen or the walls of your offices or brick-and-mortar stores. This book is about finding the galvanizing purpose that leads to greater possibilities.

A Blueprint for Transformational Success

Gui

Companies become iconic by earning the public's trust. For Walmart Mexico and Central America, known as Walmex, our model was set by Walmart in the United States. The original Walmart, founded by Sam Walton in 1962, was a retail business built on the premise that customers deserved to shop for all their needs at a store that offered them high-quality products at affordable prices. When I was named the new CEO of Walmex in January 2016, it was an honor, but it was also humbling. Not only was I going to lead this wildly popular chain of stores, but I was also asked to navigate the corporation through the biggest transformation it had ever experienced since Walmart Mexico first opened its doors in 1991.

As you'll read in these pages, it wasn't always "smooth sailing"—more like riding rough waters at times. I had naysayers who resisted, and my own emotions threatened to get the best of me. But what kept me going, despite the daunting mission ahead of me, was knowing that I had the opportunity to make a positive difference in the lives of millions of our customers. Just one thing had to happen—I had to get this whole thing right.

Luckily, I was not averse to risk; in fact, I've been told I thrive on it. One of the members of my team, Juan Carlos, says, "Gui, you take more risks than anyone I know." It may just be that I love a challenge and the chance to rise to the moment. In this case, I was resolute from the beginning. Whoever I talked to, whatever groups I met with at Walmex, I said the same thing: "This transformation *will* happen." Was it blind faith? I don't think so. It was instead a firm belief in a company that had already proven its ability to succeed. As Faulkner observed, we just needed the courage to look toward new horizons instead of allowing ourselves to be stuck in the "safety" of the past. The one thing I never lost sight of was Sam Walton's vision of being customer-centric. That was the goal that informed every key decision I made in the tempestuous months to come.

Gui

When I first began thinking of the transformation, I knew that even though my vision for change was hazy (at best), I needed to trust my instinct to take the company into the future by leveraging technology—to become fully digital to be successful in the age of e-commerce. If you are not prepared to act, to take *risks*, you die with the vision and the company dies with you.

I started with the basics. What seemed like minor changes to me were seen as radical by others in a traditional company like Walmex. For example, when I learned that only top executives had keys to use certain private bathrooms, I said that needed to stop. From that point on, every bathroom in our offices became accessible to everyone. Some said I was dismantling an entrenched hierarchy that had existed for decades. Perhaps I was, but my intent was simply to achieve a more equitable HR model, breaking down walls so that everyone would feel respected and have equal access. In the transformation to come, the power of all of us working together—of building an interdependent cohesiveness—would be a lesson we would learn many times over. And it would be a key to our success.

Carlos

The specifics of Gui's vision weren't evident at first to anyone, including Gui himself. He couldn't provide crystal-clear messaging when his ideas were still hazy at best. Nevertheless, I knew Gui's instincts and intuition were not only strong but would be laser-focused on what could be—*the possibilities* for the future that would ensure growth and sustainability as the company evolved from its original purpose. I also knew that, given human nature, Gui would meet resistance from those who simply wanted to keep on doing what was already familiar to them. And Walmex was not just any company. Like Walmart, it was a trusted retailer and a vital presence in many communities throughout Mexico and Central America. People counted on them, and a transformation could not afford to damage that trust.

Gui

The magnitude of the size of Walmex made a complete transformation a formidable task. We had 6,000 people working at our corporate offices and more than 230,000 in our stores. They were still celebrating the success we had achieved the previous year. People were proud of achieving their targets, and they were also very happy with the bonuses they received as a result of their efforts. So, there was no desire for anything to change.

This was not the kind of environment I had encountered at previous companies. Throughout my career, most of the changes I had participated in were related to improving businesses that were not doing well or restructuring companies that were in countries going through an economic crisis. This was the first time I was leading a transformation of an organization that had been doing well for decades and few saw any discernable need or urgency for transformation.

In addition, I was new to the company in Mexico, and having just arrived I had not yet built up enough credibility with my team to propose a major change. Also, I had not identified specific goals so I couldn't yet articulate a clear vision of what had to change.

Early Years: Gui's Path to Success Before Walmex

Gui

My path to becoming a CEO was not always easy. At the start of my career I was working in finance at the large multinational company Unilever Brazil during a hyperinflationary period (80% monthly inflation), and I quickly began to acquire respect from senior leadership as a result of a system that I developed that would automatically recalculate our margins by region whenever there was a cost increase. After five years I was suddenly transferred to the United Kingdom to work in Unilever's Head Office, where nothing I was doing appeared to be important or urgent. My first year there was very frustrating. I was young, had never lived abroad, and did not speak English very well, but I was intensely ambitious and courageous. When I arrived in the United Kingdom, I soon discovered that my limited proficiency in the language made it a challenge to fully understand what my boss was telling me. I kept this a secret, fearing that my lack of fluency could hurt my career. Looking back, I'm sure people had already figured this out, but I was so stressed out about it that it caused me to feel a constant emotional paralysis. The following nine months were the worst ones in my career as I suffered quietly, trying to hide my problem. In the end, my own performance suffered, and for the first time I felt like I was in rough waters being pulled out to sea with no lifeline in sight.

When I was at my lowest point, my previous boss from Unilever in Brazil, Humberto de Campos, came to visit the central offices in London and invited me to dinner. There was something about his wise, gentle manner that made me feel I could open up to him. When he asked how I was doing, it was as if the dam inside me suddenly burst: I blurted out what was going on and apologized for letting him down. "You're the one who fought to expatriate me, and all I've done is make a mess of it. I don't know what to do—I'm frustrated with myself for not doing better, for not living up to your belief in me."

His reaction was completely different from what I expected. "I'm sorry to hear this, Gui, but I'm not surprised you're feeling stressed. It's very difficult to do a great job at Head Office, where all eyes are on you. Have you done any traveling? Or something to distract yourself and clear your mind?"

I shook my head. "I'm not in any mood to travel or have fun," I replied. I knew that no matter what else I did, it wouldn't change the facts of this situation.

I must have been in worse shape than I even knew; the sympathetic concern in his eyes told me so. "It's a mistake not to be open to possibilities," he said. "One of the most important things I did during my expatriation time was to travel, to learn about different cultures. Just try to get through this period, even if it means doing the bare minimum at work. When you return to Brazil, I'll make sure you get a good job."

The following day he came to my house and had a long conversation with my wife and me. It was incredible the way he managed to calm us down, to show us a different perspective of the situation. "This is simply a time for learning," he counseled. "Try to worry less about proving yourself—you've already done that to me—and instead spend time getting to know new places, try new things. It's a way for you to also learn more about yourself."

Soon after that, I had my annual appraisal. My UK boss, John Ripley, asked me if I wanted to say something first and I decided to reveal everything that I was feeling: the words just tumbled out. I didn't feel I was being productive or doing anything useful. Because of my lack of fluency in English, I often couldn't understand him or what he wanted me to do. I was disappointed in myself, and I was sure he was disappointed in me too. "I just feel like I should give up," I said. "I'm not used to feeling like this . . . I normally work hard and produce good results but, in this situation, I feel like I'm not able to keep up . . . and I don't even know how to do better."

After listening intently to my struggle, he said, "I'm grateful to you for being so open and sincere, Gui. And I'm sorry I didn't do more to check in with you, and to give you the help you needed." Instead of chastising me, he helped me feel I was truly being heard and gave me credit for speaking up. We had an honest, in-depth conversation and by the end of it I felt reassured. In clear terms he explained what he wanted me to do, laying out a step-by-step plan of action, and he even said he would help me reach my goals.

I worked hard to make progress on my English, to see my lack of proficiency not as an obstacle but as an *opportunity* to do better. Fortunately, my will won out over my weaknesses; I was resolved to master the language or at least become fluent enough to prevent that from being a barrier, and I did. Language can create walls or open doors, and I was determined to open as many doors as I could for myself.

After my appraisal, I had two great years and my London boss became a mentor for the rest of my career. I promised myself that I would never again suffer quietly or pretend that I was fine when inside I felt that everything was going wrong.

This is a lesson for anyone reading this book. If you feel there is something wrong with you or your performance, the best way to deal with it is to confront it. By trying to hide it, you are only making the problem bigger and delaying action. You become unhappy and everybody sees it. The thing to remember is that everyone has good and bad moments, everyone falls at some point, but the ones who succeed are those who get up and take the time to figure out why they fell. Learn from the past and move on.

Carlos

This illustrates how sometimes we do not realize how our own internal dialogues may be feeding our insecurities to the point of turning them into debilitating forces. The way we talk to ourselves becomes an internal transmission of our thinking about ourselves, part of the identity we assume.

The American poet Maya Angelou puts it very succinctly: "The real difficulty is to overcome how you think about yourself."

Gui

Many years later, when I received my first appraisal in 2004 as Global Head of M&A in London from the Global CFO Rudy Markham, he told me I had done well during my first six months, and he set high expectations about my future at the company. Instead of feeling happy that all my hard work had paid off and my dreams were coming true, my stomach was in a knot. I revealed to Rudy that I'd been experiencing a lot of anxiety and even having panic attacks. "I think I should retire," I said.

He replied, "What's happening to you is not so unique. Try not to worry so much. You don't need to know everything. And remember, mistakes are allowed." He told me that even if I made some error that had negative consequences, he would never think I was unprepared for the job. "Just relax," he said, smiling reassuringly. "You've already passed the test!"

His words meant a lot to me. He helped me to see that the main problem had been the pressure I had been putting on myself. I was much more concerned about what I had expected from myself than about what others expected from me. I wanted to grow, to do big things, and had this idea that I needed to learn and deliver great results 100 percent of the time. I didn't know how to let myself off the hook, to just relax and stop worrying about trying to be "perfect."

I remember that one day I made a small mistake and then I spent days trying to fix it. Rudy told me to stop, turn the page, and forget it. He said that by trying to fix one mistake I was making another one: "Stupidity is something that grows and gets compounded. You have lots of credit to spend due to the good work you've done. You normally deliver and that one mistake is not going to change that. But you've got to move on."

It was great advice, and from that moment onward, my life changed in powerful ways. I learned that I was in command of my life, and that it was better to confront a situation instead of letting my fears make it worse than it really was. Intellectually I understood that I didn't need to be perfect to succeed, but it was a lesson that would take me years to accept deep within. However, I did feel freer to make mistakes or at least to admit it when I didn't know something. When I relaxed, I started to learn faster too.

Twelve years after I had the conversation about my career with Humberto de Campos, my boss from Unilever Brazil, I had my first job as a CEO, heading up Unilever's subsidiary in Mexico. The company had had seven CEOs within the previous ten years, and it had just experienced one of the worst years in its history. I was so happy with the promotion that I didn't stop to think whether I had what it took to lead a turnaround. Maybe it was my own youthful confidence, but I believed that just working the way I always had would be enough to help the company succeed.

In those early days as CEO at Unilever Mexico, an interviewer asked me what the most difficult thing was about being promoted to the top position. My answer was that all my mistakes would now be public, and that people would realize I made a wrong decision even before I did! As CEO you can no longer fly under the radar; everyone is looking at you to see how you'll react. When you make a blunder, you have three basic options. If you look up and act like you did nothing wrong or, worse, that you don't care, people will say you're arrogant, particularly if you try to place the blame on others. If you look down and appear to be embarrassed, they think you're a loser, especially when you try to correct a mistake and end up making an even bigger one. I used to compound the problem with my old habit of seeking perfection; the more I tried to be perfect, the worse I felt when I wasn't. The third option is the best: accept you made an error as soon as possible and try to learn from it. Instead of looking up or down, look ahead and move on.

The first six months were not good (*again*!). I felt that I had to fix every problem I encountered, that no one on my team should rest before every issue had been addressed, and that hard work would be sufficient to change the future of the company. Which just shows how much I didn't know.

As I discovered, there was a lot to learn. The company was still not where it needed to be, and neither was I. I was lucky that four things happened that reversed the course of our downward spiral.

First, I learned the value of prioritization. My boss informed me that the company had hired a consultant to review its go-to-market operations globally and offered me the pilot operation to test the methodology. Initially I thought it would be a sign of weakness to accept the offer, but the realization that we were failing helped me to see it as an opportunity to improve and so I accepted the offer.

The first phase of our pilot operation was to assess the current situation of the business. As a result, we came up with a list of more than 40 issues that had to be fixed or improved. The methodology allowed us to choose only four and this was very frustrating as I hated to see any problem go unaddressed. But the fact was I had been taking on too much and giving similar importance to a variety of different types of issues. In trying to fight all the battles, I ended up not winning any of them. So, we chose only four initiatives, based on the level of impact they had on the business and the right sequence to implement the change.

The following 12 months were more successful. By focusing all our attention and resources on a discrete number of issues, we were able to come up with solutions for all of them. We felt so powerful that by the end of the year we selected 10 additional problems as our next set of priorities. It was no surprise that we had a hiccup. When we saw we were starting to fail, we had to once again pull back and focus on fewer issues. Once again, by narrowing our focus, we scored more tangible wins. By the time I left the company, our team was one of the best performers in the whole organization.

Throughout this book we will highlight important lessons to help leaders succeed. One of the first lessons I learned at Unilever Mexico was the importance of pivoting and adapting when I realized I had taken on too much. It came down to making choices about what needed to be done most versus what we wanted to do or thought we should do.

Prioritizing is a key condition for success. Our strategy was about choosing what we would *not* do as much as what we would. In the process, there were debates, trade-offs, and concessions, but that whole process yielded the most effective results in the end.

Prioritization helps an organization focus its energy on the few things that will deliver most of the results. I have learned to lean into the Pareto principle that states that 80 percent of the consequences come from 20 percent of the causes. The problem is that hardworking people often have a difficult time separating what is important from what seems urgent. Urgency demands attention, but that doesn't mean it's one of the essential priorities that will help you achieve your desired results.

Some lessons take time to learn. Right before I was promoted to CEO of Unilever Mexico, I had taken part in a development seminar based on Bill George's book *True North*, where I was asked to define my legacy as a leader. I wrote that I wanted to be known for leading winning teams and for helping everyone in the company fulfill their maximum potential so that they would personally benefit from the company's success. I had worked very hard my whole career to get this job, and once I started, I worked even harder to improve the business and deliver on what I saw as my legacy. There was no doubt in my mind that I had to pursue my goals with every fiber of my being.

Luckily, at this time, John Ripley, who had been my boss during my first expatriation to the United Kingdom back in 1993 and was now a valued mentor, came to visit me. He is a dapper, distinguished-looking man, one of the most intelligent people I have ever met, an excellent boss, and an exemplary human being to whom I will be eternally grateful. He was about to retire and, given his years of experience, I wanted to know if he thought I was moving the company in the right direction and if there was anything he thought I could do better.

During his visit I learned another lesson from him that helped me change course and lead the company to success. He told me that he was confident I was taking smart actions to turn around the company but that by working 24/7 I was inadvertently "forcing" my team to do the same. He said, "This is *your* dream, and you're happy to do it, but have you asked your team if they also want to give up everything else to deliver your dream? Have you given them a different option? Is it really necessary to do it this way?"

It was because of John that I learned an important leadership lesson— everything we do affects other people. It is the ripple effect in action. Not only was I working too hard, I was causing others to do the same without even realizing it. John helped me to see that my behaviors were neither right nor effective in the medium to long term. I could tell he was reluctant to call me a "workaholic" because I knew he considered himself one too. But that made his words even more powerful—he was urging me not to make certain mistakes that he had made in his own career.

Carlos

Being the first to arrive at the office and the last to leave is no longer considered a badge of honor. On the contrary, it's perceived as a sign of inefficiency and poor self-management habits. Work is an important part of one's life but it's not everything; balancing a fulfilling professional life with a satisfying personal life is the healthiest equation.

In her *New York Times* best-selling book *Thrive*, Arianna Huffington writes of the April morning in 2007 when she experienced a startling wake-up call. She was lying on the floor of her home office in a pool of blood: "On my way down, my head had hit the corner of my desk, cutting my eye, and breaking my cheekbone. I had collapsed from exhaustion and lack of sleep."

She was at the top of her field, on the cover of magazines, and "had been chosen by *Time* as one of the world's 100 Most Influential People. But after my fall, I had to ask myself, was this what success looked like? Was this the life I wanted?"

Later in *Thrive*, Huffington states, "We think, mistakenly, that success is the result of the amount of time we put in at work, instead of the quality of time we put in."

Gui

The two concepts we've discussed above are very much related: lack of prioritization and working too hard. Try to fix everything at once and you will work hard and fail. Even worse, you will believe that life is unfair as you are not being rewarded for all the hard work you're putting in to fix the past mistakes of others. Leaders should provide clarity about where to take the company, and decide the priorities they want to set. If they don't, others at lower levels of the organization will make those choices themselves in an uncoordinated way, and the result will be catastrophic. In the same way, working too many hours is neither healthy nor productive. By focusing on fewer things—not taking on a herculean workload—you will be able to work smarter and generate better results.

The third fortuitous thing that occurred was that I had a series of conversations with Vinicius Prianti, the CEO of Unilever in Brazil, who had been my boss when I was CFO there. Vinicius had invested a lot of time showing me the importance of knowing our customers and consumers. He invited me to meetings with our clients and really expanded my view of business beyond the numbers and P&L. He also showed me how to delegate. The more progress I made, the more responsibility he gave me. He was an inspiring boss, a great manager, and a person I profoundly admire. I used to phone Vinicius every week during my first few months as CEO in Mexico, consulting with him about my vision and strategies. It was his attentive listening and support that gave me the confidence I needed at the time. He always finished the conversation by telling me, "You are prepared and you will make the right decisions when you need to make them." He never told me what to do, which was probably easier for him, but he helped me to grow.

During those conversations there was one other thing Vinicius used to say that stayed with me: "As long as you deliver your targets, you'll have the freedom to do it your way."

I began to see what a profound concept this was. That delivering my targets was a long-range strategy for gaining the credibility I needed to act on my vision—and achieve buy-in—for moving the company forward. Delivering on a target must not be a matter of trying to negotiate to reduce that target. If you have open, fair, and transparent discussions during the initial, target-setting phase, you'll get the respect and trust of your bosses. I never understood leaders who want to show their bosses the great work they've done but when the subject of targets comes up, all they want to do is complain about the difficulties and risks the business faces. They attempt to lower expectations, anticipating the possibility that they won't be able to meet their targets. This behavior generates distrust, and you cannot lead a transformation unless your bosses trust you without reservation.

The fourth factor that helped us succeed at Unilever Mexico was that we hired Carlos Marin to coach me and our leadership group. Carlos helped us to become a fully integrated team, and to think in new ways about how we were performing. We became a stronger, more united team with a clear strategic focus while developing talent as we never had before. Carlos was also helping me to change personally. I stopped being so obsessive about everything and learned to be more focused as a leader, concentrating on the strategic issues of running the company. I realized that my job was about trusting others and asking the right questions rather than depending only on myself and trying to come up with answers to solve every problem. By defining the critical goals we had to deliver, I became a more effective leader, the team became more cohesive and energized, and ultimately the company was successful.

I began to crystallize a formula that became my leadership credo: *define your key priorities, work for success but not to excess, focus on fewer issues—making sure they're the most essential ones—and deliver what you promise.*

Carlos

Essentially, much of my focus with Gui at Unilever Mexico had to do with revisiting and putting into practice things he already knew—for example, applying his laser-sharp vision of success for the company, establishing and communicating clear priorities and sticking to them, and setting an example for his executive team as I helped them become more integrated and work collaboratively. I recall the executive team deciding on four priorities to address and then, within a short time, that number had doubled. So Gui's challenge was not only to help set priorities but to make sure the company maintained a steady attention on them as *the most important results that needed to be accomplished.* We agreed that instead of fighting the demands of what seemed urgent—but was not strategically very relevant—he needed to concentrate on attaining the goals that had been set with the resources he had available.

The Beginning of the Walmex Transformation

Gui

After four years as CEO of Unilever Mexico and two-and-a-half years at the helm of Walmart Brazil, I was named CEO of Walmex in January 2016. I knew the scrutiny would be stronger than ever before. But at least I felt I was ready; I had worked hard over the years to stop searching for perfection and instead be more open to learning, evolving, and adapting.

At the beginning of my career, I wanted to be admired for the quality of my work and to prove to my bosses that I had explored all angles of a problem to come up with the best solution.

I felt driven to dedicate a lot of time to working hard, studying long hours, even earning a business PhD. However, I was always worried about messing up, which caused a great deal of anxiety. When or how would I make a mistake? I never felt I was truly good enough, and this was the quickest route to unhappiness. It took me a long time to realize that being perfect—getting things right all the time—was simply not possible; it was also not relevant to being successful. Perfection is a lifelong quest, not a destination.

Carlos

A negative side effect of perfectionism is the need for external approval. The lessons for any leader are to discover her or his purpose, nourish their capacity for self-approval, and listen to the whispering instinctual voices within.

Being aware of their internal monologues or silent conversations can help leaders reflect on and process their external experiences privately. Given Gui's history of striving for excellence and his belief that "perfection is a lifelong quest, not a destination," it was important for him to notice how his thoughts affected his actions as a leader.

During our coaching sessions, I encouraged him to pay attention to his inner monologues about what was happening around him and to determine how these thoughts affected his emotional reactions. I also challenged his thinking and explored ways to arrive at different and hopefully more effective conclusions for his role as CEO. The aim was for him to have positive responses to the question: "How well am I doing on my journey toward continued improvement?" Better awareness of his own internal monologues became a helpful tool for Gui to use.

The positive aspect of perfectionism involves using it as motivation to do your best, set high standards and realistic goals, and strive for improvement by learning from unexpected outcomes. These pursuits require significant energy levels. Gui had to manage his tendency to push himself so hard that he tested his endurance to the limit.

Gui

The idea of transforming Walmex first took hold early in 2016. Our business in Mexico and Central America was having another great year both in terms of growth and profits, and we were doing much better than our main brick-and-mortar competitors. However, emerging e-commerce competitors were moving faster than us, and it looked like a whole new wave of digital-native businesses were coming at us from all sides.

Though I was enthused about the potential of technology to revolutionize our business, I also felt daunted by the huge amount of work ahead of us. I'd been through enough challenges before to know I had to keep calm and focus. Prioritize what we needed to work on first. *Don't worry,* I told myself, *you will make this happen.* I reframed the way I was looking at the situation; instead of seeing all the advances being adopted by other companies as a big threat, I chose to view this moment as the biggest opportunity we would ever have to grow Walmex's business.

As I began to realize what was happening in the world—exponential technologies, digital transformations in business—what once seemed impossible now looked inevitable. We could move from a world of scarcity to one of abundance, where the way we offer customer service would be totally reimagined. Having Walmex become digitally enabled was not only a necessity—it was an *opportunity*.

I started this journey alone. Because I couldn't stop talking about the need to change and wasn't very clear when I tried to articulate this vision, many people were initially put off. But there were also those few who "got" how momentous it could be if we applied technology to every part of our business.

Though many naysayers believed we were wasting our (and their) time talking about "futuristic fantasies," some of my associates and I delved deeper into our research—reading about technology, sharing what we learned, meeting tech-savvy experts in the field, and thinking a lot about how to transform our company. We saw that, in this changing world, if we continued to be the same, one day we would run into a wall. Although we continued to deliver great results, I sensed something was missing from our business equation or, to put it more positively, there were rich opportunities just waiting to be seized.

Just as I didn't allow language to be a barrier to my own progress in my years in the United Kingdom, I was firmly resolved to become tech-literate, once again to see my lack of knowledge not as an obstacle but as an opportunity.

I was determined to learn as much as I could about how to leverage advances in the field to ensure Walmex's competitive edge. We would combine our new digital tools with a vision rooted in Sam Walton's original mission to help people save money and live better, and to always put customers first.

The book *The Infinite Game* by Simon Sinek inspired me. It changed my idea of how to measure success. I learned the difference between a short-term view (which was the one I had used for many years) and an infinite, long-term view. According to Sinek, "Great leaders set up their organizations to succeed beyond their lifetimes." He also said that "in an infinite game, the primary objective is to keep playing, to perpetuate the game" and that "we need to think about how to build organizations that are strong enough to stay in the game for many generations to come." That was exactly what our founder, Sam Walton, did so brilliantly. It was what I knew I had to do for the future of Walmex. At 50 years old I decided that this would be my legacy: helping to transform a large and successful company into a much better one.

Gui

And then, just as I was excitedly beginning to plan for Walmex's transformation, I received my second-year appraisal from my boss. As I wrote earlier, it was as if he had dropped a bomb, and suddenly my self-confidence was shattered. What made it such a shock was how unexpected it was, given the impressive results we had achieved. My call to Carlos in the early spring of 2018 was an urgent plea for help: I felt like a drowning man in need of a lifeline.

Carlos

Gui and I had worked well together during his time at Unilever Mexico and more recently as I prepared his team at Walmex for the transformation. I could tell from the urgency in his voice how serious the situation was. And there was something else—a deep pain and bewilderment that I had not heard from him before. I assured him that I would do my best to help him.

Gui

I felt the negative appraisal had to be the result of people with ill will and dubious intentions trying to attack me. I assumed that Carlos only needed to intervene with the team to make things right . . . I could not have been more wrong.

Carlos

Because I was already working with Gui's team in support of the transformation, I knew he was admired for his genuine, contagiously passionate energy, known around the company as the "Gui Factor." This inspired and attracted people from inside and outside Walmex to form a growing cadre of enthusiastic collaborators.

My 30 years of experience as an executive coach working with global leaders have taught me that the leader must set the stage for any major transformation, identifying and clearly articulating the actions they want to take to move the organization forward in new directions. I also understood that change is uncomfortable for people who don't want to be taken out of their comfort zone. I felt the best way I could help Gui was to find out how his mission to transform Walmex was having an impact on him and his associates and to help them navigate the process.

Of course, I immediately agreed to coach Gui while continuing to work in parallel coaching his team. At the time I had no idea of the kind of tumultuous journey it would be or that I'd have to draw on all my years of training and my experience in the field of executive leadership development to be the coach he needed. But there was one thing I was sure of: I would do the work required to fully understand the situation and to work with Gui to develop a plan to successfully address the issues that had surfaced.

Gui

I just didn't know that one of those issues would be *me*.

LEARNING POINTS FOR SUCCESSFUL LEADERS

Reinventing Yourself to Transform Your Company

Reinventing Yourself

- **Lesson:** As a leader you'll want to cultivate a desire for learning and to see opportunities and possibilities where others see only difficulties and impossibilities. A sense of curiosity and wonder will allow you to reframe challenges as potential solutions.

  > "Every great dream begins with a dreamer. Always remember, you have within you the strength, the patience, and the passion to reach for the stars to change the world."
  > —Harriet Tubman

- **Lesson:** Focus on your top priorities, giving critical attention to the resources you'll need to attain your strategic objectives. Work for success but not to excess, and you'll serve as an example of efficiency for others in the organization to emulate.

  > "We must use time wisely and forever realize that the time is always ripe to do right."
  > —Nelson Mandela

- **Lesson:** An important factor in self-improvement is for you to gain awareness of how the inner monologues you may be having with yourself could be affecting your behavior. Such self-talk could range from optimistic encouragement to discouraging criticism that may be self-defeating and stifling. By being mindful of their impact, you can choose to cultivate the more positive side of the continuum.

  > "Make sure your worst enemy doesn't live between your two ears."
  > —Laird Hamilton

- **Lesson:** Wise leaders recognize the benefits of having someone with more experience to advise and support them throughout their career. Try to find a mentor who will help you learn and find the strengths that may be hidden within you as you move forward on your journey.

> "The delicate balance of mentoring someone is
> not creating them in your own image but giving
> them the opportunity to create themselves."
> —Steven Spielberg

Transform Your Company

- **Lesson:** Transformation may involve a major disruption in the status quo as your company becomes more agile and resilient in the ways it serves your customers and coworkers. As the leader of such major change, you'll want to inspire the openness, trust, and transparency needed for everyone to collaboratively tackle the challenges that will inevitably occur.

> "You never change things by fighting the existing
> reality. To change something, build a new model
> that makes the existing model obsolete."
> —Buckminster Fuller

- **Lesson:** Prioritizing the needs of your customers and employees will provide your company with a greater chance for success.

> "The biggest driver of sustained growth
> is the client experience."
> —Virginia M. (Ginni) Rometty

2

"If It Ain't Broke"

"Individually, we are one drop. Together, we are an ocean."
—Ryunosuke Satoro

Gui

When you're running a company that's exceeding expectations and you tell everyone you want to make massive changes, the objection you hear the most is: "Why tamper with success? If it ain't broke, there's no need to fix it."

I understood their point of view. We had all worked hard to deliver a banner year, bringing in sales that exceeded all expectations. If anything, my team wanted to get some time to catch their breath. To bask in the glory of a job well done. Not to rest on their laurels but certainly not to dive headlong into a potentially grueling upheaval of the company's essential operational systems. Why make life so difficult when we were enjoying reaching a new peak of success?

The answer loomed large for me. Every day, I was reading about digital-native businesses that were leveraging technology to give us a run for our money. Like a photographic image that gradually begins to develop when submerged in a chemical solution, the picture of our future became clear to me. As one of the most iconic companies in the world, we had the trust of our customers. But we had not invested in the kind of technology necessary to help us compete against the rise of other companies that were well positioned for the world's rapidly growing digital economy.

In this chapter we will take you back to the earliest days that preceded the start of the Walmex transformation in 2016, to show you how I realized that the company needed to prepare for change but that I wasn't yet aware how to effectively communicate the need for transformation to the very people who had to implement it.

––––––––––––––––––

My first day at Walmex in January 2016 taught me a lot about the company. I arrived in Mexico and my boss took me directly to an off-site meeting with the top leaders of the company. We drove together to Cuernavaca, known as "the City of Eternal Spring," the lush capital of Morelos, close to Mexico City. We did not talk about business during the journey, and I felt good (if a little anxious) about my new role and having the opportunity to dive into the deep end to begin my position as CEO.

Luckily, my boss was more relaxed than I was and with good reason. Walmex had bounced back the previous year with a stellar performance after a few difficult years that nobody had expected. Ever since becoming CEO of Walmart Brazil in September 2013, my dream had been to run Walmex, the largest retailer in Mexico, and a company that was known for putting people first. Unfortunately, the first time I was asked to lead the company, at the beginning of 2015, I had to say no as family issues prevented me from making the move. It was important for me to stay with them in Brazil rather than relocating to Mexico. But the delay worked to my advantage—I was now coming to a company that was riding high, having already turned around its performance from the difficult years of 2013–2014. It also had its own way of doing things, relying on tradition, structure, and a command-and-control corporate culture.

What did my boss see when he glanced at me as we made our way to the off-site? I imagine he thought I had the confident stride of a leader who felt honored to be taking over Walmex—but I was not as self-assured as my boss may have thought. Perhaps he caught a glimpse of nervousness in my eyes, the apprehension that comes along with assuming more responsibility than I'd ever had before.

The meeting went well as executives defined the strategies to put into action for 2016. I sat back in my seat, feeling I could relax and just observe the way others were presenting. They were doing all the work and it seemed that for my first meeting I could get away with nodding and smiling and giving the speakers my full attention. And then, as the meeting was drawing to a close, my boss asked me to speak to the assembled crowd.

I had not prepared anything, and in that moment I knew it would be best if, as I usually do, I spoke from the heart. Heading to the front of the room, I looked out at the faces of the many people I would come to know well, but whom, in that moment, were still strangers, looking up expectantly at me to get their first sense of who would be leading the company they all cared about so deeply.

I started by saying, "Congrats on a great 2015. We are back in the game. Because of your efforts we are again beating our competitors and delivering our targets. We are back where we belong—on top!"

Applause came in waves, getting louder and louder as I looked out at my new colleagues. And as the clapping subsided, I felt compelled to be honest.

"But," I stated, "I believe we are missing something. I believe we can do more for our customers. Don't get mad or ask why this is my gut feeling. As a Brazilian I love soccer and I believe we are like a team that can beat the opponent ten–zero, but we are happy with one–zero. Let's work together to win ten–zero."

The next second seemed like an eternity as I surveyed the reactions. I do not consider myself arrogant, but when I believe wholeheartedly in something, I believe in taking a huge leap, even if the risks are great. Nothing less will do. I had made a leap of faith, taking a risk that I would not play it safe just to make a good first impression. In that moment of suspended silence I think most people were so shocked by my comments they just stared at me, perhaps not knowing how to respond. Did they think I was chastising them? The fact was I believed enough in them already to challenge them to do their very best. Some of them I had met when I was CEO at Unilever Mexico and they knew I admired them. We had enjoyed doing business together. They were now the first to nod and smile, to see my words as a demonstration of trust that they could achieve more. As if the entire room was exhaling, there were more smiles, more nods, more understanding that I was urging them to do better because I was certain they had not yet tapped the best they had to give. The applause that followed was more thunderous than before.

The following week, one of the vice presidents for the company that I knew when I was a supplier came to my office. He sat uneasily in the chair across from me, and from the tense, deliberate way he spoke, it sounded like he had spent time rehearsing what he would say.

"Gui, I admired the work you did when you led Unilever in Mexico and so I was confused by your message at last week's meeting. We had a great year and presented an ambitious plan for the company's future. So why do you think we need to do more?"

I could tell he was trying to understand my thinking, and I did not want him to feel I was undercutting all the efforts he and his fellow team members had made. "My friend," I replied, "I believe that our values and talent here at Walmex can take us well beyond what is in our current strategy. We can do even more to help people save money and live better. I still don't know what is missing but I would love it if you'd help me find the answer."

Though I was reaching out to him, I felt he was stuck in the feeling of wanting me to validate what he had done in the past rather than becoming a partner with me to search for new ways of doing things for the future. The VP's jaw tightened as he spoke. "Do you believe we didn't do a good job? Our results have been outstanding—we are recognized by the entire market as having the top talent. Why do you have a feeling we can do better?"

He was reframing my position, as if I was saying they lacked something when instead I felt that it was their abundance of talent that could be used in more strategic ways to benefit our customers. "I respect the past of this company," I said. "I'm not criticizing it, and I'm not talking about randomly shaking things up just because I can. What I'm saying is that we need to honor our company by improving it, so it can continue to be successful. The best way I can honor my predecessors is by encouraging Walmex to achieve its full potential. Doing good is not good enough. I'm not being paid to do good but to help the company achieve the greatness we're capable of."

The VP leaned back in his chair as if relaxing for the first time since we started speaking. "I see. So, we don't need to get scared about a new boss trying to change things just for the sake of change?"

"No way; no one should feel scared. I believe the best time to promote change is when we are doing well. We shouldn't wait until the business starts to decline before we start to think about transforming the company to be more competitive. There is a lot we need to do to keep pace—and surpass—the digital-native businesses that are champing at the bit to advance against us. I'd like for you to join me in being part of this mission."

I saw a flicker of understanding in the VP's eyes that told me he was seeing *why* we needed to create the future I was talking about. He leaned forward and said, "Gui, you can count on my support. I'm in."

I must confess that though I admired this man, I never would have guessed that he would be the first person to buy into the transformation. He came into my office ready to forcefully challenge me and he was leaving as a fierce advocate. I hadn't shifted my position or presented specific details for what needed to be done, but in the time we sat speaking a seismic reversal had taken place. The VP shifted his point of view because he heard four data points that made a difference: 1) his job was safe, 2) our company, *whose success he had contributed to*, was not safe given the competitive forces aligning against us, 3) we could not afford to wait to take action, and 4) I trusted the team could deliver the transformation.

For leaders who will find themselves in a similar place in the future, think about the value of seizing the moment to reassure colleagues that transformation is not a threat but an opportunity to work together to bring about an even more customer-centric company. I realized in that short meeting that as the leader of Walmex, my job was to counteract the fear that comes with change by emphasizing the promise and possibilities that are part of it too. I invited him to join me because I knew he would be an effective partner in the upcoming process. I was asking him to be part of our transformation without defining his role—only letting him know he would have a role. I relied on a simple fact: if we care about maintaining our success, we have to care more about satisfying our customers.

Whether the VP realized it or not, I was removing the sense that this was about him individually; it was what the company as a whole needed to achieve—it was a mission bigger than any one of us, including me. In this one short meeting I was beginning to crystallize the early outline of what it would mean to be a leader in a time of change. There were a lot of answers I didn't have, which would result in some mistakes down the road. I didn't yet have the words to articulate a message that would inspire all the people I'd have to bring with me. But what I did have was resolve and a rough draft of what the company's transformation meant for everyone involved—those of us who were part of the company as well as the customers we served. Whether I could persuade everyone to become advocates was an open question. But this one small victory at least gave me a glimmer of hope.

Carlos

Change can be scary and uncomfortable for people and pushback is a predictable reaction to it. When someone presents new ideas that disrupt the status quo, a natural reaction is for others to defend their position and hold their ground. Being able to manage this "knee jerk" response is an important, practical skill for any human interaction, and especially if you're in a leadership position. But what does it take?

Like mastering any skill, this one requires constant attention and practice. These are the areas to focus on most when having these types of conversations:

- Maintain your composure by staying calm, centered, receptive, and respectful of how the other person might see the situation.
- Listen carefully with an open mind and without interrupting the other person.
- Suspend judgment, keeping your own biases in check as you hear what someone else is saying.
- Verify you understand what the other person's concerns are by offering a summary of what you heard them say.
- Ask questions to seek clarification of the person's viewpoint.
- Thank the person for sharing their perspectives (recognizing it's not easy for them to push back against the boss). Assure them that you both share the same intention and similar goals: to do what is best for the organization.
- Find common areas of agreement, looking for ways to invite the person to be a contributor, as Gui did so brilliantly in the scenario above.

Gui

One of the change agents we hired to help us move the transformation forward was Eduardo de la Garza, who joined us as senior vice president of HR in 2018. He saw the kind of opportunity he would have to help us improve the associate value proposition (AVP) of our company, which had more than 230,000 associates. By helping our associates embrace digital technologies, he would transform their careers and future. He would positively impact not only their lives but the whole labor market in Mexico and Central America.

Eduardo de la Garza, Chief Human Resources Officer, Walmex

I had been at PepsiCo for 32 years in high leadership positions, on their board and loving the company. I had no reason to leave this global company. And then Gui got in touch with me and invited me to his house for a private conversation about joining Walmex. He said he wasn't trying to sell me on the new position. He simply wanted to show me his passion.

"It's not going to be easy," he said. "The transformation of the company is going to be demanding."

I wondered if this was the right moment for me to make such a change, and then Gui said something that stayed with me:

"Things will be intense but what you do will have an impact, improving the quality of life of our 240,000 associates."

I was impressed by Gui's spirit as well as his knowledge and intention. He was also direct. "I'm ready to make you an offer. I want you to be my copilot on this journey of transformation."

He invited me to be a special guest at a shareholder meeting so I could get a sense of Walmex's culture. I attended and I also got a sense of Gui's passion for people. There is a particular word I use: *cherish*. Gui is a leader who cherishes people, whether it's his employees or his customers. He wants to make a positive impact on their lives, and that is unique in my experience.

Of course, I said yes to Gui. At the time, my wife asked, "Are you really sure about this?" I told her I was. I had never been so excited. Gui earned my trust and I don't have a single regret about joining the company.

The Business Battle of the Century

Gui

When I first came to Walmex, I hit the ground running, attending to the daily issues a retailer faces as well as trying to build a strategy that would take us to the next big win. But even at this early stage I took a pause and asked myself, *What does a big win mean?* For years I always thought it was about growing the business, increasing market share, increasing profitability, distributing bonuses to associates, and being happy with the achievements. In my first year at the company we beat our competition, improved profitability, paid great bonuses, and our engagement survey improved, so I had all the reasons to be a happy CEO. However, as I had said at my first off-site meeting, I felt something was missing. We were scoring more goals, but somehow I knew this was not enough.

Two things occurred while I was working hard to figure out how Walmex could do better. First, I began to explore what was happening in the retail industry in the United States and Asia, two markets that were more advanced than Mexico. Steeping myself in research, I had the opportunity to learn more about the strategy of new digital players and how they were changing the dynamics of retailing to consumers. When I saw how traditional companies were trying to counterattack start-ups that had more technological savvy, I realized that we were part of the business battle of the century.

Second, I was invited to spend a day at Singularity University, based in Santa Clara, to learn about the impact of the digital revolution. I was curious about what I would discover but I didn't have huge expectations—though that was due more to my lack of knowledge about the work they were doing than anything else. This was my first exposure to all the new digital technologies that were having an effect worldwide and I learned how to leverage them to become more competitive. I didn't expect to get such a far-reaching and comprehensive overview. The faculty experts spoke about the changing possibilities of what could be done in every area, from medicine to agriculture to expanding knowledge. The deluge of information made me wonder: *How soon could all these developments become a reality?* It was impressive to hear that innovation was occurring at a speed unheard of just a few years ago. The seemingly impossible was becoming possible overnight.

I was fascinated by what I was learning here versus what I had been taught in the past, a divergence that was often surprising. At Singularity University, the experts talked excitedly about "a world of abundance" whereas for so many years I had heard we were living in a world of scarcity. Here, they confidently promoted the idea that we were close to having "free energy" even though I could only think about the constant rise in energy prices. They emphasized a computer capacity that was well beyond my imagination, certainly beyond anything I had seen at any company I knew.

Another idea that fascinated me was their concept of "exponential companies," about how things start small and suddenly grow dramatically. They talked of a new world in which innovation was the rule and not the exception. Horizons that had not even been imagined yet.

I always loved the idea of building a better future, but all the information I took in on this visit also convinced me that the disruptions Walmex would face getting there could be more monumental than I had initially suspected. I was excited about what we could accomplish, but at the same time I was intimidated by the scale and speed of the changes we'd need to make.

After our one-day session, I came back home very energized and sat down with my wife, Patricia, to discuss my trip. We had both studied business at the same university and, although we worked in different areas, we loved sharing new ideas. As we opened a bottle of wine, I couldn't hide my enthusiasm—or my fear. I bombarded her with a barrage of details I had learned and then she asked me the one question that had been on my mind, too, but that I had avoided thinking about because the implications were so profound.

Quietly, she said, "What does it mean for the way you'll lead Walmex?"

"I don't know, Paty," I replied, not having a better answer to give her. "I don't know how we'll apply these new technologies to Walmex's business. I have so many questions. What systems are best for us? How do we use them to serve our customers? I don't even know what I don't know or what I need to learn."

"Don't worry about what you don't know now," Patricia said. "I know you and I'm sure you'll do your best to prepare for all this."

"You know I love challenges," I said. "I love to confront difficult situations and I'm not scared about the risks of the unknown, but . . ."

"But?"

"This time is different," I told her. "The unknowns are bigger. And there are more challenges than I've ever faced in my life before. At the same time, I believe this is the biggest business opportunity in my career. I want to be part of this astonishing new world and not just sit back and watch it happen. I want to dedicate the time it takes to understand everything."

Patricia could sense my worry, and what she said has stayed with me ever since. "Gui, you have prepared yourself for this moment your entire life. You've got to go for it!"

She said she wanted to learn with me, to figure out ways she could apply the technologies to her own business. We were so excited about the possibilities we drank the whole bottle of wine and neither one of us could sleep that night, given how wound up we were!

It's About the Journey

Gui

When the President and CEO of Walmart, Doug McMillon, decided to visit us later in 2016, I saw this as an opportunity to share my ideas with him about why it was important for Walmex to proceed with a top-to-bottom transformation. He had already begun to lead a major transformation for other divisions of the company, including in the United States, and I felt it was essential for us to get the green light to start one for Mexico and Latin America. The reason for changing globally was clear, but a strong case needed to be made for why Walmex, which had been doing well, required a substantial investment of money so we could remain competitive.

I was eager to learn from Doug, given his vast knowledge and experience as Walmart's global CEO. While I was proud of our company's results, I was eager to promote my ideas for transformation and to impress upon him why we needed to move quickly on all fronts—bringing Walmex up to speed technologically, retraining our staff, and creatively identifying fresh ways to enhance convenience for our customers.

In our company, we don't usually go to the airport to collect our visitors. We prefer to stay at the office working. But this time was special. I felt that having one-on-one time with Doug would help me get his undivided attention before he began the day's busy agenda, which did not include the topic of transforming the company.

It was early in the morning when I started the trip to the airport and began rehearsing the points to make when I spoke with him. When he arrived, he was surprised I was there to meet him. Given the travel time, I knew I had one hour to make my case before we reached the office. I launched into my comments about what I believed we needed to change in the company and why; however, looking back, I see that I rambled and did not present a concise narrative.

In response, Doug said, "Tell me about the journey you took to come up with the ideas you just presented to me."

"But wouldn't you prefer to talk about the ideas themselves?"

"No, it's your journey that interests me more," he said. I had prepared for a number of different responses from him—particularly pushback—but not this. He was patient as I stumbled my way through an answer, speaking about why I felt now was the time to be proactive, especially after witnessing what other digitally native businesses were accomplishing. I gave him only a broad-strokes picture of my journey, emphasizing only that I felt passionately about honoring Sam Walton's vision to make a difference in the lives of our customers.

"Nevertheless," I said, "I don't think we're able to be as customer-centric as we once were. In order to recover that capability, we have to become more digital and agile without losing all the great attributes that distinguish us from our competitors. I intend to change our business so we're able to better compete with digital-native companies. This will be an important opportunity to use technology to serve customers and it will be a change that affects everyone at Walmex."

I tried to convey why change was so important at this moment in time, but there was so much to say and not enough time. When we arrived at the office for the day's meetings, I was sure I had failed at the one chance I had to share my vision of a transcendent transformation with global CEO Doug McMillon. I was feeling downcast and deflated when he smiled and said, "Go ahead with the transformation. You have my permission and support."

I was not sure I had heard him correctly. I wouldn't have given my approval if I were him. "Why?" I blurted out. "How can you support me if I've been unable to clearly explain to you what I have in mind to do?"

Just as Doug was about to stride into the front door of our offices, he paused and said firmly, "Our company needs to change. I'm giving you my permission because other people who have been most successful at leading changes at their companies have had journeys similar to yours. So, go ahead."

I was amazed. Given my command-and-control background, he gave me a great lesson in leadership. Ask the right questions and give those around you the freedom to excel. By putting his trust in me, he motivated me to do my best and to trust myself as I determined what needed to be done.

Transformation Lies Beyond the Comfort Zone

Gui

At first I took it for granted that if I said we needed to invest in a technological realignment, my team would "get" it even if they weren't quite ready for what that shift would mean, financially, structurally, and, most of all, emotionally.

But ultimately I realized that as technology evolved faster, every company would seek to use more of it at a faster rate, but that alone was not the solution. Our transformation would need to be about changing the way we worked more than anything else. The technology would not really be effective unless our executive committee also grasped the need to function as a collaborative, interdependent team, anticipating and addressing the needs of our customers.

My enthusiasm in charging ahead didn't help. You can't expect people to run with you if they're still not sure why they should be in the race in the first place.

I remember at the beginning, I would simply say, "Trust me. We need to transform the company to maintain our competitive edge," but I was unable to clearly articulate what we needed to do or how we would take a strategic approach to managing this large-scale transformation, which would radically upend our company's culture as we knew it. I didn't understand the ramifications myself, so how could I expect others to grasp them?

I felt like I was on this journey alone, but soon I found a few people on my team who seemed eager to join me. One of them was Leticia "Lety" Espinosa Vera. Lety is a digital-native person with an entrepreneurial DNA and a desire to better serve our customers. She grasped my vision, even though it was hazy at the time. When I asked her why she was ready to trust me when I had so little information to share, she talked to me about her digital mindset and willingness to help Walmex change. She said, "What you want to do, but haven't yet been able to formulate in a clear way, is what I want too. Let me be part of the team that defines it." Later I saw a sentence on Lety's LinkedIn page, which seemed to sum up the kind of fearlessness required of anyone who was going to be part of this mission: "Transformation lies beyond the comfort zone."

I didn't fully appreciate the anticipatory fear many people were feeling. Without specific details, it's natural for staff to think the worst or to be dismissive, preferring not to consider that change was really looming on the horizon, as if the idea of transformation were "Gui's folly" that soon would pass.

As I mentioned in the previous chapter, before I continued with my plans to implement such a massive, company-wide transformation, I decided to ask executive leadership coach Carlos Marin, who had been immensely helpful to me at Unilever Mexico, to step in and work with my team, to prepare them for the changes ahead.

The "Success Trap"

Carlos

When I initially met with the vice president of HR and her staff, they briefed me on Walmex's current leadership team, in preparation for my work with the company's senior vice presidents who formed the executive committee (known as "Exco"). I learned they had much to celebrate and be proud of—business results had been outstanding. The teams who reported to the Exco were highly regarded professionals in their respective areas of expertise, with each unit independently evaluated and earning bonuses based on whether they achieved their own assigned performance targets, therefore promoting a way of working that did not incentivize interdependent collaboration.

It soon became clear to me that their mindset was: If working in silos was leading to record results, why change? The positive assessments and bonuses they had received only reinforced their commitment to preserving the status quo of operating as they always had. However, I believed this situation defined the classic "success trap," where an organization is willing to continue exploiting their current business activities while neglecting to explore new ways and possibilities to ensure more viable, long-term success.

This represented a strategic opportunity for members of the Exco to improve their ability to collaborate and work in partnership with each other, especially in anticipation of the impending transformation Gui was conjuring up for the company. My goal was to help them lead and behave more effectively as executive vice presidents and directors of the whole company and not just senior managers of their own individual business units. I believed this consequential shift in thinking could lead to new synergies and the exploration of potential growth options.

The Walmex HR team contracted with a consulting company to conduct a comprehensive 360-degree assessment process that would identify strengths as well as opportunities for individual and collective improvement among all the vice presidents and senior vice presidents who were members of the Exco.

A few years before, in October 2008, I had assisted Gui and his HR team at Unilever in a very similar way as they conducted a comparable assessment of their senior leadership team. We helped them recognize their key strengths and identify ways to increase their performance and cohesiveness as a leadership team. It was because of Gui's experience with the development work I had done with their executive team, helping them communicate more effectively, refocus their critical business priorities, and become more accountable, that he recommended me to his HR partners at Walmex. He had witnessed how we achieved positive results by emphasizing personal growth through behavioral change. In a transformation, Gui understood that it wasn't only operations that needed to be reimagined—it was his team's view of themselves and their role within the company that needed to change too.

I delved into the 360-degree report to see what I could glean before I spoke with the Exco team myself in a series of individual telephone interviews. The consulting firm described the executives as "knowledgeable," "experienced," "confident," and "adaptable," willing to make changes in the organization as needed. But there were warning signs I detected as well: the existence of organizational silos prevented an exchange of common experiences and valuable information across departmental boundaries. In group discussions they tended to veer away from their main objectives, focusing instead on tangential, less relevant details that made them less efficient or effective.

According to the report, there was often excessive questioning of new ideas, which implied mistrust of other team members who were seen as slowing down project advancement and made interactions more cumbersome when dealing with problems. I was not surprised to read that these issues were accompanied by defensive attitudes, like finger-pointing and blaming other teams when things went wrong. The command-and-control structure encouraged competitive behavior and undermined team cohesiveness. Senior leaders were rarely encouraging of one another and did not often offer positive recognition for good performance. Overall, relations were described as formal and somber. I realized I had my work cut out for me—time was of the essence and I needed to help them build collaboration and trust among team members who were used to working independently if Gui's transformational vision was going to succeed.

I felt at this time I had enough data to help these executives embark on the first step of a "Transformational Learning Journey," in which they would build on their strengths and identify areas for improvement that would allow them to be a more cohesive and even more effective leadership team. In June 2017, I asked my friends in HR to set up virtual interviews with each member of the Exco. By establishing one-on-one conversations, I'd be able to introduce myself, explain my role, and listen to their views about themselves, the company, and their perception of Gui in his role as CEO.

My plan was that after meeting with them virtually, both individually and as a team, I would ask HR to set up an off-site in-person meeting that I would facilitate. It would be the next step of our "Transformational Learning Journey." My questions were: *What would happen if the issues mentioned in the assessment were positively addressed? Could the company continue to be successful considering the evident challenges arising from new technological advances and competitive companies manifesting themselves in the marketplace?*

Based on the team assessment reports and my own virtual interviews, I had arrived at conclusions about what I saw as senior leadership's strengths as well as their opportunities for improvement. These points would provide me with a road map for designing the off-site workshop.

Primary Strengths:

The group is task oriented and committed to achieving results. In addition, they are:

- Experienced professionals with ample levels of technical expertise in their specialty areas.

- Self-confident and willing to make autonomous decisions based on their own criteria.
- A flexible team, capable of readily adapting to changing demands in the marketplace.
- Open to challenges and enjoy participating in projects that will help the company grow.
- Able to genuinely accept feedback if it benefits the development of the company.

Primary Opportunities for Improvement:
Senior leadership reveals overall insufficient coordination with other areas of the business, with their silos causing execution problems further down the organization. Other issues include:

- Perceived variation in how performance is evaluated, with some feeling that bonuses were based on varying performance metrics. In other words, some interviewees felt that performance was not being evaluated with the same yardstick across all areas of the company.
- Individual actions are valued and rewarded over collaborative efforts.
- Lack of accountability and regard for how individual decisions impact other areas.
- Subdivisions of groups that include expats vs. locals, Gui's direct reports vs. those who report to International Headquarters.
- Avoidance of mistakes and control are highly valued and rewarded.
- Considerable self-protective behavior and finger-pointing to avoid responsibility for errors.
- The executive committee lacked a well-defined and cohesive purpose and mission.

When it came to their perceptions of Gui, there was a diversity of opinion, ranging from positive feedback that he was "very approachable and sincere," with "effective interpersonal skills" and having a "strong intellect" and "passionate enthusiasm," to suggestions for improvement. Some felt that his emotionally charged responses hindered effective communication and that he needed to be more structured and better organized. There were also concerns that his "informal and casual" approach as the company's CEO did not align with the organizational culture and could be misinterpreted.

The Off-Site Meeting: A Transformational Learning Journey

Carlos

In July 2017, all the Exco senior leadership were invited to attend the off-site, which would include a series of experiential activities that would help these highly professional individuals coalesce into a team.

Before the meeting, I asked each team member to reflect on their own strengths and attributes and areas for potential development and then to do the same for their colleagues. I gave them a two-part pre-off-site assignment: The first part focused on questions about their strengths that had been helpful to them professionally and asked them to define how they could be even more effective in their current role; the second part asked them to identify "important behavioral characteristics" of every colleague on the Exco and then to provide constructive advice to each one of them individually, with suggestions that would benefit their ability to contribute to the team's overall success. I was hoping these probing questions would lead to new levels of openness and that the meeting would be a Transformational Learning Journey that would result in more cohesive leadership.

Gui

The transformation we wanted to implement at Walmex required us to focus on the customer and to deliver better and faster solutions to them. As a result, we had to stop working in silos and start to think of creating a more collaborative, cooperative environment with an end-to-end view. Before the off-site began, I wondered what possibilities we could achieve if we could all work better together.

Carlos

The participants arrived in the morning at the Camino Real Hotel Sumiya, a beautiful, Japanese-style hotel in the city of Cuernavaca. I entered the hotel excited about the interactions that were about to occur, the insights that would be shared that would prepare everyone for Walmex's transformation.

As we all gathered around the designated conference room tables that were arranged in a U-shaped format, there was a natural sense of expectancy in the room.

Gui

Carlos asked me to open the meeting, and I wanted to transmit to the team how excited I was about our future.

"Good morning!" I said. "First, I want to congratulate you and your teams and to say thanks for the results we have achieved in the last eighteen months. Yes, that's how long I've been here, and I appreciate the way you welcomed me and did so much to achieve the goal of helping our customers live better.

"I told my boss the other day that working for Walmex is like going to Disneyland. I love my job and have never faced a situation like the one we have now: we're a company that has done well for decades, but we still have the opportunities to improve and the resources to help us do that.

"The best resource we have is our people. We are the top leaders of this company and we should be proud of what we're achieving. But we can have an even greater impact on the lives of our 230,000 associates and six million customers who shop with us daily.

"We are starting a transformation in our way of working, and the first change is about eliminating the barriers and obstacles the silo organization imposes. It's a structure that our company and many others have used for years, organizing teams in terms of specialized expertise. But in order for us to have an end-to-end view of the needs of our customers, we have to have a full under-standing of the problems they face. That means a shift away from silos. Instead, we need to work together in a more collaborative way to focus on customer pain points and to design and implement sustainable solutions. It is about behavior, and this begins with the way this leadership team works.

"So here we are today to get to know each other better, to connect to each other and appreciate all the exciting things each of us has to offer as well as to let each other know how we can build an even better team and a better company. Carlos helped me to lead a huge transformation in the company I previously worked for some years ago. He is a great professional and is very keen to work with us. So, now that we're ready to begin, I want to thank you again for your leadership and for participating in this off-site. Let's make history together."

Carlos

After Gui delivered his opening remarks, I expressed gratitude to everyone for their participation in the interviews that we had conducted earlier. I emphasized that the insights they shared had been very helpful in designing the activities I had planned for the next few days.

I then added, "There are a few things I'd like to request from everyone to help us make this a successful executive learning experience. Please be fully present—and by this, I mean body, mind, and heart. Your contributions and active participation are fundamental. There will be active opportunities for you to interact with each other. Therefore, listening to each other and practicing 'judgment suspension' will help you better appreciate your own and your colleagues' situations and points of view. The main goal for these two days will be for you to return to work knowing you made important progress toward becoming a more integrated and effective senior leadership team for Walmex."

I invited the group to move to another part of the room where the chairs were arranged in a circle. To start the session I asked everyone to sit in silence for 30 seconds, and to simply experience being calm; I wanted them to relax, and to let themselves "arrive" and be there.

Once everyone seemed settled, I began to speak: "Sitting in a circle this way changes the group energy significantly. There is no end or beginning. Everyone is visibly present. For centuries humans have gathered in circles to share information and learn from each other."

I provided prompts for the group to speak about, sharing their own experiences using various topics like where they were born and raised, where they liked to visit or go on vacation, and who was a person that had a positive influence on them.

As they interacted, I could see them grow more and more relaxed. The level of group harmony and comfort slowly increased as each person's stories and values mirrored those of their colleagues. Their comments flowed with an openness and spontaneity that I had not witnessed before among the team. The key was that they were speaking from the heart—not about what they did professionally but who they were personally. They had become at ease with each other and were able to compare how others perceived them in relation to how they viewed themselves.

We also discussed the concept of "the comfort zone," the psychological state where we feel secure, in control, and confident as opposed to feeling vulnerable, exposed, or susceptible. It's the place where we can feel productive. However, I made the point that if we hope to learn and experience self-development, we need to stretch and expand our comfort zone into a "grow to perform zone." This does not mean we have to demolish our comfort zone but instead make it more extensive. As Patrick Lencioni says in his book *The Advantage*, "At the heart of vulnerability lies the willingness of people to abandon their pride and their fear, to sacrifice their egos for the collective good of the team."

This was the crucial next step in our Transformational Learning Journey—the group had established a newfound intimacy, which would help them to more effectively participate in a one-on-one private conversation activity. This involved everyone pairing up with a partner according to a previously assigned matrix to act as peer advisors, offering constructive, honest support as they practiced listening with open minds and engaging in constructive conversations. The goal was for them to help their partner improve as a member of the Exco. In particular, I suggested that each person focus on an issue they wanted to work on in themselves and to ask their partner for feedback.

I developed this experiential activity to have an impact that would transcend the walls of this off-site setting. I gave them directions that would provide important parameters for their one-on-one conversations:

- Be respectful, positive, and respectfully supportive.
- Suspend judgment, be receptive, and listen with an open mind.
- When offering suggestions, provide specific examples to help your partners gain a clearer perspective.
- Take notes and observe the time to give your partner equal opportunity.

As this activity progressed, I could see how the animated participation and camaraderie among the pairs was gaining momentum. It was as if there was a change in the room's emotional temperature as people shared openly and listened attentively. They were expanding their comfort zones and growing to perform within this new, psychologically safer space. When we debriefed the activity afterward, people shared some of their newfound realizations. Many in the group found that the barriers to communication and collaboration had occurred as a result of self-imposed assumptions, such as the fear of appearing "weak" or "vulnerable." Others said they had never before sufficiently appreciated the value of interdependence as an executive team. One of the striking epiphanies was that so many others shared thoughts, feelings, and opinions that were very similar to the ones they had. Finally, they expressed the importance of making time to constructively work on themselves and learn from each other. It was clear that they saw the benefit of investing in personal and professional growth as a means to greater collaboration, especially as the company was on the verge of a major transformation.

The last activity took our Transformational Learning Journey from this off-site meeting to the real world of working at Walmex. It was a rubber-meets-the-road exercise where participants had to write about how they would translate the information they obtained in this workshop into concrete, actionable results back on the job.

I asked everyone to select one specific and significant leadership behavioral challenge that they would be willing to commit to work on, one that would result in improving how they performed on their evolving executive committee. They had to create a multifaceted plan with a specific objective, identifying the steps they would take to achieve it in the next six months or less. Among the areas they needed to consider were:

- Potential barriers that may get in their way—what are they and how will they address them?
- One or two colleagues they'd like to reach out to for additional support. Who are they?
- Resources they would need to draw on to reach their objective. What are they and how do they plan to obtain them?
- What are the key indicators that would demonstrate they had accomplished their objective?

Once everyone was done, they were asked to join two other colleagues to form a triad to go over each other's plans, to make sure they had met the established criteria. Each person then projected their plan on a screen and shared

a summary of it with the rest of their colleagues for a final review and validation. This activity reinforced the experience of collaborating with—and learning from—each other, recognizing they all had areas they wanted to improve.
Our sessions over the past two days had prepared them to trust their colleagues
enough to seek feedback and suggestions from them. Executives who had been
used to working in separate silos were now reaching out to others, finding common ground, and seeking to provide help to their peers. In this off-site, we had
built a foundation for more effective communication and collaboration within
this fine team of executives.

As we finished up, I wondered, *Would the group be able to convert the progress
they made over these two off-site days into a sustainable new way of working on-site?*
I knew only time would tell. But I was hopeful the changes that took place here
would carry over. I saw I was not the only one who felt that way. As I was pack-
ing up, I glanced at Gui, who smiled enthusiastically and gave me a thumbs-up.

Gui

As I confronted the enormous task before me of transforming the company, I
realized that I had two missions: to preserve the essential DNA of the company,
the core values and principles of helping people live better that stretched all
the way back to founder Sam Walton, *and* at the same time change people's
way of working—their behavior—as we became a digital, agile company that
could achieve new levels of sustainable success for the future. Our DNA was
the reason we existed, but reinventing our behavior would allow us to search
for excellence to honor Sam Walton's original vision in innovative ways. As we
moved forward, we had to help our customers feel the improvements without
having their shopping experience negatively altered by the flux and upheavals
that we would inevitably go through as we made operational changes. It was a
balancing act that would require everyone's attention and best effort.

From a Leader of Internal Support Services, Walmex

Change is driven from the top, and people were looking to Gui to
see how he would help a hierarchal, risk-averse company embrace

---

transformation. He taught us that evolution is a constant and we can't afford to be complacent. The company shifted away from a command-and-control model and Gui helped us all learn an essential lesson: that by sharing the decision-making responsibilities and listening to others, you don't lose power but gain strength.

Gui

With Carlos coaching my senior leadership team, I felt comfortable that they would bring their A-game to the mission, even if it meant changing their own work habits. Years ago, I had read the book *Now, Discover Your Strengths* by Marcus Buckingham and Donald O. Clifton, PhD, who put forth the idea that instead of spending time and effort trying to fix the weaknesses of people we lead, we should instead focus on improving their strengths. I loved the idea and remembered that during the many appraisals I underwent (and all the ones I did for my direct reports), more time had been spent discussing weaknesses rather than strengths. The authors argued that by focusing on strengths we could help an individual reach their maximum potential, which would benefit the company as well.

I supported this concept and valued it as a breakthrough approach to personal development. But slowly I was beginning to see that I was using it as an excuse to avoid dealing with issues that I needed to address. I was delaying the work I needed to do to be better. For too long I had assumed the attitude, *This is who I am—take the good and the bad.*

As I observed Carlos coach members of my team to look more closely at their behavior and change the aspects that weren't benefiting them or the company, I began to wonder: *Was I refusing to step up to the plate, to challenge my own behaviors that were no longer proving to be effective?* I had discovered my strengths, as Buckingham and Clifton had advocated, but did I now need to give equal time to my weaknesses? It was a passing thought, but at that time, as the CEO facing the transformation of an iconic retailer, I felt the transformation of the company was more important than my own personal reinvention. In the months that followed, I would come to realize how interrelated both transformations were.

LEARNING POINTS FOR SUCCESSFUL LEADERS

Reinventing Yourself to Transform Your Company

Reinventing Yourself

Success requires different capabilities in different times and situations. What made you great in the past is not necessarily what is needed to help you achieve a successful future.

You should use your strengths to help you overcome your weaknesses and to give you the confidence to make changes. You don't want to be stuck in the status quo, justifying your current way of doing things as a reason not to change.

- **Lesson:** Know who you are and what makes you unique. What are your strengths, your capabilities, and passions? Be ready and willing to learn how to be even better than you are now.

> "Do not let what you cannot do interfere
> with what you can do."
> —John Wooden

- **Lesson:** Embrace your calling. Listen to what the whispers of your heart are suggesting—it could be your purpose.

> "To change the world around us, we
> need to change ourselves first."
> —Santosh Joshi

- **Lesson:** Expand your comfort zone. Be willing to part with old and familiar ways to jump into new possibilities, despite how scary that can be.

> "Life begins at the end of your comfort zone."
> —Neale Donald Walsch

- **Lesson:** Be an avid and humble learner. Ask and be open to receiving help and support from others.

"Listen to feedback, be open to change, leverage
your strengths, accept your limitations, be persistent
and never lose sight of your vision."
—Saskia Sorrosa

Transform Your Company

If you want to be a great leader, you'll need to challenge *and* support your team, trusting and encouraging them to move ahead. Find the people who support your vision, and give them more responsibility to bring your company to its full potential.

- **Lesson:** Know your customers and develop a deep understanding of how to exceed their expectations.

    "There is only one boss. The customer."
    —Sam Walton

- **Lesson:** If your company is doing well, that's the right time to make it go for great.

    "It's very easy to be different but very difficult to be better."
    —Jonathan Ive

- **Lesson:** Attachment to success in the past can get in the way of a company's success in the future.

    "You can't move forward if you're still hanging on."
    —Sue Fitzmaurice

- **Lesson:** Change is the breakfast of performing companies.

    "The biggest part of our digital transformation
    is changing the way we think."
    —Simeon Preston

3

Perform to Transform

"It works if you do the right thing the right way."
—Fábio Barbosa, CEO, Natura & Co.

Gui

I believe there is a fine line between a genius CEO who is transforming a company and a weak CEO who is distracting the company with unnecessary changes. The fine line is called quarterly results. You are as brilliant as your last P&L.

After my first year, I knew I had proven myself—the fact that under my leadership we had exceeded expectations in sales and profits meant that I had earned the credibility necessary to advocate for an unprecedented transformation of the company. It wasn't something I just *wanted* to do but something I knew we *needed* to do, given the technological edge that other digital-native companies had over us. They hadn't caught up with us yet. But they could and would if we didn't take drastic action.

This chapter is not only about how I had to prove I had gained enough credibility within the company to lead change, but that I also had to be humble enough to recognize what I didn't know. The transformation of a company, like personal reinvention, requires deep questioning and learning. In my case, it was about how my team and I had to rethink our approach to our customers and our associates, most particularly their pain points and how to solve them. My learning curve also involved being aware of who our competition was and the advantages they possessed so we could know what aspects we needed to strategically develop most within our company to sustain and even increase our customer base.

The pace of the digital revolution was slower in Mexico than it had been in the United States and Asia so we were able to see how companies that were technologically savvy were having a huge impact on the retail business in other regions. My colleagues in these countries helped me identify the threat of digital-native companies:

- They established a digital relationship with customers that allowed them to better understand their preferences and buying habits. Digital-native companies had also become adept at pinpointing customer pain points and resolving them more effectively than us.
- They were simplifying the lives of their customers. For example, Uber helped people order a ride with the press of a button, and Airbnb made it possible to find lodging just as easily. E-commerce companies provided quick access to a wide assortment of goods and services at low prices, with products delivered wherever the customer wanted.
- They were able to monetize their relationship with customers through advertising.

The new companies were better at collecting data about customers because they had the technology to build a digital connection with them. They knew them better and could communicate more effectively with them because they understood more about their needs, habits, and pain points. They were also faster at offering solutions to their problems. That's what motivated us to change—to gain more data, improve our insights, and be more agile, end to end.

The more customers you attract to your site by selling advertising, the more that sellers want to invest in advertising on your site to convince customers to buy their products. Digital companies started to sell advertising at a much higher scale than their brick-and-mortar competitors and so they were able to generate a lot of resources that could be reinvested in lower prices, which could result in more profits for them.

It was obvious that we'd soon be facing digital-native companies that would use these advantages to fight for market share of customers. I felt we needed to see the potential we had at Walmex to compete. We were already ahead of the game in some respects—having a long-standing brand meant we already had a substantial customer base and relationships we could monetize in a variety of ways; the new businesses first needed to acquire customers in order to monetize them. If we could become digitally savvy and use agility to respond more effectively to our customers' needs and pain points, we could be a formidable competitor to the digital-native companies that were emerging on the scene. But at this early stage we hadn't yet generated ideas about what we could accomplish—that would only come over time as we learned more about our customers and increased our capacity to implement actions that would serve their needs. We didn't have a moment to sit back and rest on our laurels.

A boss and dear mentor in the company I worked at before coming to Walmart used to say that delivering your targets gives you the freedom to operate. When you do what you promise, your boss will rarely interfere in your business.

As I was contemplating the transformation of Walmex, a friend who had been nominated to be the global CEO of a large consumer packaged goods company told me about his predecessor. "He was always trying to transform to perform, and after many quarters of sales results not meeting expectations he was fired. I'm going to take the exact opposite approach: perform to gain the right to transform."

His words resonated with me, and "perform to transform" would become one of my core mantras as a leader. I knew that by delivering positive results in my first year I had earned the right to transform. And as a company we had to transform in order to continue to perform in the future.

I began having frequent meetings with our leadership team about what change would look like for Walmex. Some team members had a fixed agenda, focusing more on our continuing to meet results, while others wanted to speak specifically about issues we would need to manage during the year. When I had the chance to meet with my boss, he already knew I felt we had to become more competitive with digital-native companies. In one conversation in particular he wanted to know what they were doing that gave them an edge.

I responded, "It's easier to provide you with some examples. Last-milers are able to deliver faster and better than us, our website is more difficult to navigate, and our competitors offer a wider assortment of products. We have not yet made the online shopping experience as convenient as the top e-commerce companies."

My boss encouraged me to tell him more.

"These other companies are frankly better than us at understanding and solving customer problems."

"I understand and agree," my boss replied. "What and how are you planning to move on?"

"It's still not clear to me," I said. "But I know we need to start experimenting with things like becoming more digital and agile, acting on customer pain points as we discover them. We can make a start and see where it takes us. The business is in good shape and I believe some of us can dedicate time to this."

My boss nodded. "Your results are great. I trust your team will not take the focus away from our core mission in order to develop some of these new ideas. But you and your team have earned the right to experiment. Keep me posted."

This go-ahead from my boss would never have happened if we were not already delivering our targets.

Changing the Mindset, Not Just How We Work

> "The most valuable thing you can make is a mistake.
> You can't learn anything from being perfect."
> —Adam Osborne

Gui

I grew up in a generation where a product was only put on the market when it was considered to be in perfect shape, so it took me some time to realize how e-commerce was shifting the goal posts. The edge that start-up digital-native companies had was not only technology and speed—it was their comfort level with putting out products that were not perfect at all but were good enough. In my case, my adult children were the ones who first taught me this lesson.

I wanted to replace my tablet but I was wary of getting the newest model on the market given the bugs it would probably have. I was leaning toward a slightly older model that would presumably have the early problems fixed.

"Dad," my kids groaned, not even trying to hide their exasperation, "get the model that's just come out. Yes, it's going to have bugs but it's still going to be much more advanced than the previous version. You'll get more options, more power, more speed, and the manufacturer will fix the bugs over time."

This was a mindset alien from my own, but it was clear that I was the outlier here, not my children. The world had shifted to accepting a "good enough" product as good enough. It wasn't only a change in technological advances that revolutionized our culture, it was a change in mindset.

Walmex is not simply a retailer; every year we produce thousands of new products, partnering with many vendors to design and manufacture everything from electronics to clothes, from toys to home furnishings. It is one of the main ways we are able to offer customers items at an affordable price.

However, if the customer mindset was transforming their buying habits, it meant that we as a company needed to change our own mindset as well. It was as much of a priority as learning and implementing technology. This was an early "aha" moment for me. I realized that it would be impossible to lead a transformation in which we became a more customer-centric, creative, and agile company if we did not rethink how *we* thought about working. Unless we adopted a new way of innovating and serving our customers, we would never be able to compete with digital-native companies.

We had asked our teams to utilize agile methodology to solve some of the problems they were confronting, but when I went to one team presentation of a new product, the executive committee (including myself) asked hundreds of questions and spent hours suggesting lots of different solutions. At the end of the meeting, I noticed the team that was presenting to us was very confused. We had inundated them with questions as if they had to have a perfect solution ready—and at the same time we were encouraging them to experiment. Since Carlos was now coaching me, I felt it was important to hear his thoughts about the meeting because I didn't feel I had led it properly.

Carlos

Our conversation started with me asking Gui to recount what had happened.

Gui replied, "As you know, in order to test our new way of working, we have formed some multidisciplinary teams to experiment with working in a more agile way. Today, one of those teams presented their first findings and proposed initial actions and we tortured them with lots of questions and flooded them with suggestions."

"What was their reaction?"

"All of us on the leadership team got more and more excited about the work and started to generate lots of ideas and asked for answers they didn't yet have. I could tell they were confused and probably frustrated because they were getting mixed messages from us. They had been tasked with piloting a program of agile working, where their goal was to learn about customer pain points, formulate a few ideas to solve them, test those solutions, learn which ones were most effective, perfect them, and then test them again. Instead of allowing the team to proceed as they had been instructed, we were asking for conclusions even before they had started to test the initial ideas."

"What did you say or do then?" I asked.

Gui replied, "I knew our behavior did not help the situation. After a lot of debate among the leaders, I told the presenting team to go ahead with their proposal, to consider some of the points we had raised, and to keep us posted."

"Did your leadership team discuss how they experienced the meeting?"

"Some of them came to me later," Gui said. "They felt we had not handled the meeting very well and I agreed with them."

"Gui, what did you take away from the experience?"

He reflected for a moment and then said, "The meeting was not a good one but it resulted in a great learning opportunity for us. We discovered it's not enough to design and plan change. Each of us has to change in order to earn the right to lead the transformation."

Gui

Our transformation required us to digitize our processes to understand and serve our customers better in addition to learning to be agile to deliver faster solutions to them. Both objectives demanded that we see and act with an end-to-end mindset. To do all this, we needed to work differently. We knew how to do it, but it wasn't always easy to change our behavior overnight. It was an important wake-up call for us.

Carlos

A key coaching point to highlight is that Gui and his team became aware of ways to make these presentations from their teams more productive and inclusive for the future. Failure without learning is a wasted opportunity.

I recommended to Gui that after the next presentation, he try an "After Action Review" (AAR), which is a lively, straightforward, professional discussion of the meeting that had taken place. It is an excellent chance for all participants to reflect on what happened and contribute by sharing their observations and insights to improve future team presentations.

An AAR is not a place to criticize, disapprove, or complain, but rather, to listen to what all the participants have to offer, regardless of their title, position, or rank, as they respond to the following questions:

- What were our expectations for the presentation?
- What actually occurred?
- What went well and why?
- What can be improved and how?

Gui

Carlos's coaching helped me to understand how one action or attitude means more than thousands of words. In this first project meeting I felt that the executive committee and I had behaved in a totally command-and-control style, exactly the opposite of what we said we would do. We would never make progress if we spent so much time on discussion rather than development; we had to let go of trying to take charge of every aspect. As leaders we needed to concentrate on "the what," and the multidisciplinary teams had to have the freedom to define "the how."

Ultimately, we told the team to experiment with their ideas, and the process moved faster than it would have if we became mired in endless talk about refining every detail. We helped them understand that product design and testing no longer needed to take as much time as it had in the past and that we could bring items to market even if they were not "perfect."

This shift in focus would allow associates to embrace a greater degree of agility as they developed products. Our transformation would need to progress on parallel tracks—changing our own employees' minds about their work habits while at the same time transforming our operational abilities to leverage technology.

For us to have an impact on leadership's mindset, we needed to take a top-down approach, with employees taking their cue from me. They would have to see a change in my mindset—that not only was I embracing technological advances but *the way I thought about work* and the development of our products. My team needed to see that I was trading my own perfectionism for a belief that, like more digitally native companies, we could serve our customers better by producing items that could be refined over time. Customers benefit by getting products sooner without waiting for exhaustive testing to green-light them and bring them to market.

To lead change, it's necessary to be courageous. If things go wrong, the CEO will be blamed first. But being courageous is different from taking unnecessary risks. I knew that to move forward I needed to discuss the transformation with a diverse range of people, listen to different opinions, understand the possible outcomes, and define what kind of support would be needed and from whom. Based on the advice of others, I had to feel free to change my mind; only a foolish person remains rigid and unbending when presented with options that may be better.

There is no space for heroes or big egos in major transformations. Yes, we had achieved success in my first year, but I knew the danger inherent in that: when someone starts to generate great results and is self-confident, people become wary of questioning the "hero." They imbue the leader with superpowers and even the leaders themselves begin to buy into that false perception. This is very risky, but I've seen it many times over the course of my career. A good CEO should accept that they are not a superhero and that nobody is the owner of the truth. Teams make things happen. Teams can do much better than individuals working on their own. This is especially true during a transformation.

Even as the CEO I was not working independently, but I recognized that interdependence meant I had to set an example for everyone at the company. I would need to show others I was encouraging experimentation and agility. If the transformation was going to succeed and we were going to become more customer-centric, I needed to think more like the customers we were serving. And as my children weren't shy about reminding me, people were more interested in getting a new product that was better than the previous one rather than waiting for the perfect product. This was an unexpected but important part of my own growth as a leader. Like a suit that no longer fit, my ideas about perfection would need to be cast aside. And if I was asking my team to be more attuned to serving our customers and figuring out what they wanted, I would need to do the same. After all, I was seeing very successful companies with products and services that were just "good enough" doing great.

Carlos

Gui's goal in reinventing his leadership was to keep learning from his experiences during the transformation process, reflecting on the impact of his decisions, reactions from his stakeholders, and our conversations about them. I also emphasized that an essential aspect required changing people's tendency toward wanting perfection. My advice was to lead them by encouraging them to focus on generating "good enough" results, move on, and keep improving.

Falling in Love with the Problem

Gui

During the early stages of the transformation, some of my colleagues and I attended the South by Southwest conference in Austin, Texas, and came back with a lesson that would greatly influence our strategic thinking. One of the presenters, Ann Mei Chang, then executive director of Lean Impact, mentioned a concept made popular by Waze cofounder Uri Levine: that *instead of falling in love with the solution* (which had always been our default approach), we needed to *fall in love with the problem*, always trying to be aware of reducing pain points for our customers *and* our associates.

We would need to learn a different way of innovating. It wasn't enough to become digitally enabled—we had to enable a new mindset, breaking the barriers that came with our entrenched, hierarchal, traditionally structured company. Did people think I was crazy? Yes. Would I give them reason to doubt me? No. I told them that no matter what, *this transformation was going to happen.*

Understanding our customers' mindset meant I had to interact with them, get honest feedback from them, and really listen to their complaints about where we were coming up short. Once, when I was in one of our stores, a customer stopped me to ask about a practice he felt was unfair. He was upset that his shopping cart had to be checked at the exit before he left the store and he didn't understand why. I explained that this small inconvenience had a huge impact on reducing "shrinkage" from our store due to shoplifting and theft. The fact is many stores have to write off a substantial percentage of lost sales due to consumer theft. The issue has now reached epidemic proportions and most companies compensate for this by charging customers more for the goods they sell. We decided to take the simple measure of checking carts before our customers left the store to reduce shrinkage at our retail stores, which would allow us to continue to sell our products at low prices.

But his response surprised me: "Controlling the store and preventing people from leaving without paying is *your* problem. Why are you transferring that problem to me by making me waste my time at the exit?"

I used to believe that checking carts before people left the store was a small price for them to pay in order to save money on their total bill. But this encounter made me think about customer pain points and how we could do even more to reduce any inconvenience our customers were experiencing. Successful companies resolve customer pain points instead of transferring problems to their customers. In this instance, instead of continuing to have the carts checked manually, which was disruptive and caused additional waiting time, we instituted an in-store scanning system at each exit, which allowed the check of the shopping cart to happen almost instantaneously. This is an example of understanding the customer's pain point—falling in love with the problem instead of the solution—to see if there was technology that could be applied to address it.

The man who approached me in the store that day to complain about having his cart checked became a valuable asset in helping us get out of a boardroom mentality in order to see the Walmex shopping experience through the eyes of the people who count most: our customers. From the moment one of our shoppers enters our store to the second they leave it, we need to be attuned to what gets in the way of their convenience. It's not about what works for us because it makes it easier for our associates and agenda; it's what works for the customer. We often talk about end-to-end innovation, but we must become attuned to the end-to-end experiences of our customers, including how they respond to products, pricing, displays, checkout, and yes, entering the store and leaving it too.

Making Sure Not to Transfer a Problem to the Consumer

Gui

I was aware that some companies were transferring their problems to the consumer without paying attention to the consequences, and others made issues even worse by *creating* problems for customers.

Were other companies doing enough to alleviate problems that seemed baked into their way of doing business? Often, we're most aware of the problems that companies create. A personal example that may be familiar to many of you is the experience of using an ATM. It should be a relatively simple process—insert your card and get money. It was originally a great invention, one that provides a huge convenience to customers and solves the problem of getting cash quickly. But now companies are using it to create problems for the very customers they are serving. I insert my card, and every time I do, I get the same message about whether I want to buy insurance or some other product. Even though I always press "no," it doesn't matter. The message pops up.

When I click on "no" to respond to the option to buy the product, instead of taking me to the home page it asks me if I want another service. I always get irritated and say to "the machine," "*What do you think? Do you think I inserted my card to buy insurance? Is this what your customers normally do?*" After a quick moment of "dialoguing with the machine," I click the button that says "yes, I do want another service."

Once I get to the main page to make my withdrawal, the screen offers me suggested amounts that never match the figure that I almost always request. Why not individualize the program so an often-used amount immediately appears as an option? Once I get the cash I need, I'm done but the ATM is not—it asks me if I want to donate before I finish up. I once had lunch with the global CEO of the bank and his team and related how what was once an innovative convenience has turned into an irritating inconvenience, His team jumped in to explain why it was so difficult to change the current programming. And people wonder why digital-native companies are growing so fast at the expense of older, more traditional businesses!

When it comes to companies transferring internal problems onto their customers, one need look no further than the airline industry. It has turned the convenience of getting quickly from one place to another into a nightmare scenario that many of us have experienced: canceled or delayed flights that lead to a frustrating series of challenges—inefficient apps, lack of staff to help us problem-solve, and the risk of being stranded overnight at desolate airports after hours of trying to secure a voucher for food or lodging. Instead of experiencing efficient transportation, we feel cast adrift, as if the price for convenience is *in*convenience.

At Walmex, we decided to honor our founder and our company mission to help people live better by focusing our efforts on solving customer pain points instead of exacerbating them. I felt it was important for me, as the leader of the company, to convince my team to take their inspiration from our shoppers.

One of the things the company discovered was that many of our customers weren't buying online; in 2016, the internet was extremely expensive in Mexico, and they did not have computers or bank accounts or credit cards that would allow them to engage in e-commerce. Also, they were afraid to make a purchase without having someone they could speak with in case something went wrong with the process or the product. These were the pain points that were impeding them from doing the very thing our transformation was ultimately meant to encourage: to make Walmex the best omnichannel retailer. We knew that if we could be the company to give them their first access to e-commerce, we'd become their preferred online store.

Using this information as inspiration, Walmex quickly came up with a brand-new add-on to serve customers: in-store kiosks with a computer and a salesperson to help shoppers learn to become comfortable buying from us online, which would give them the opportunity to find the items they were looking for. Since our research also found that many of our shoppers preferred to pay by cash rather than use credit cards, we decided to make that one of the options featured in these kiosks. Customers could search for an item, and when they found it, they could buy it using cash as well as credit cards and have it shipped to them or the store itself. We responded to their needs and that's what mattered.

This solution addressed our customers' pain points, and though it may have seemed counterintuitive to have computers in our stores in a world where digital use at home was becoming more prevalent, once our kiosks were up and running our sales soared. We now have 1,300 kiosks in our stores as a direct result of our desire to become more customer-centric.

In addition to providing access to the benefits of the digital economy to customers who were not yet digital, we also realized that we had to help our own associates become more digital-savvy in order to make their work easier and more effective; as a consequence, it would afford them the opportunity to spend extra time with customers and offer them better service.

We had two end users to consider: the customers and the associates, and our efforts had to be focused on real-world interactions rather than theoretical scenarios. What were our associates' pain points? Were we doing enough to solicit information from them about what made their experience more challenging? To use technology more effectively, we first needed to increase our efforts to look at the one thing that mattered most: the human factor.

Carlos

In our coaching sessions, Gui and I discussed this concept further, especially the way the "internal" human factor recognizes associates within Walmex as customers of the company's leaders and managers. I pointed out that leadership needed to build empathy with our external customers as well as internally with our associates on the front lines attending to them. We had to acknowledge their pain points and address them properly. The transformation process naturally had to include identifying and resolving whatever burdensome issues they were experiencing as they went about implementing better and more effective ways to serve everyone who visits our stores.

We agreed that a large-scale transformation would have to include supporting both customers and associates. Gui told me, "Our founder, Sam Walton, had a clear view that we need to take care of our associates so they would take care of our customers. We need to be able to solve their pain points in better ways than our competitors do with their customers and workers."

Gui was very clear that the company couldn't improve service to their customers without improving service to their associates too. I knew that his very capable HR staff would be totally aligned and provide the necessary expertise and support needed.

Gui added, "We have a considerable number of associates and a magnificent mission to improve people's lives. As soon as our team understands that the transformation will equip us to achieve our goals, they'll join us for they'll see that everything is possible."

Beatriz ("Betty") Alejandra Núñez Jimenez, Chief Growth Officer, Walmex

I was approached two times over the years to work at Walmex, and both times I said no. I was working in a high-level position at Terra Networks Telefonica, where I had been for 22 years. But those first two times it wasn't Gui who met with me. The third time I spoke with Gui, and that made all the difference. He said, "Betty, we have the perfect role for you. I don't know what you'll be doing, but we'll create a role for you to help with the company's transformation."

I could tell this was a leader who wanted to make a huge difference for people. But I said, "Gui, if you don't know what I'll be doing, how will you measure my success?"

"Don't worry," he replied, smiling. "Together we'll figure it out. I want to transform this company. Create agility at scale and become more digital. I know it's the right thing to do for Walmex and our customers. I may not know the *how*, but I'm certain of the *what*."

I saw three things in Gui at that meeting that made me say yes: his humanity, his humility, and his visionary approach to leadership. Here was a CEO who could recognize that he doesn't know what he doesn't know. This is a rare quality among leaders. But he was excited about making it happen. I said yes without even looking at the financial proposal.

When I told my bosses I was leaving the company, they were not happy. "You're crazy," they said. "You're making a huge mistake—starting from scratch with another company. You'll be losing your prestige." I'll never forget that particular line, that I'd be losing my "prestige."

But I was undeterred. Gui had told me that this was the project of his life. It was important for him to create a legacy that was bigger than him. This became clear to me as we started working on the three pillars of the transformation: making the company more agile, digital, and customer-centric. His ultimate goal was to put our customers and associates first. It was an amazing moment as we set this aspiration for the company.

I was a digital-native with experience working for a digital company, so I knew I could be of help as Gui set the wheels in motion to transform the company.

He had heard people saying, "This is Gui's transformation," but he knew that perception wouldn't scale. "This is the company's transformation," he would say to everyone. Other leaders would want to take credit for achieving results, but Gui always viewed this as a "team transformation" and made sure the rest of us did too.

Gui

The idea of asking Betty to join the company and design her own job description seemed crazy, but we needed digital-savvy people like her to bring us up to speed in terms of implementing technology. She helped develop how the transformation should proceed and was so effective that she later became CEO of the series of new businesses we launched as a result of our mission's success.

Vulnerability as a Leadership Virtue

Gui

In my first few years at Walmex, there was something my team did not know about me: when I get nervous, I like to make a joke to relax myself as well as my audience. On the day of one of the first regular town hall meetings I led, I could feel my nerves getting the better of me as I walked into the auditorium where 1,000 associates were waiting to hear from me. Soon after I started speaking, I made a joke, trying to relax the crowd—and myself—but I could tell right away that it did not land.

After the presentation was over, I knew I couldn't just let this go. The following month, as I walked into the auditorium, I told someone from HR that I was going to apologize for the joke.

But the HR executive said, "Don't try to fix what you said. What's done is done and let's just hope they've forgotten about it."

"But *I* haven't forgotten about it," I said to him. As I stepped in front of the microphone, I began to speak, perhaps more quietly than usual.

"I owe you an apology for the joke I told you last month. Sometimes to control my own nervousness in front of an audience, I tell a joke to lighten things up, not just for the crowd but to calm myself. Last month it did not go well, and for that I want to apologize."

Something happened in that moment that I didn't expect—as I looked at the faces of the 1,000 associates sitting there, they were smiling and nodding as if to let me know they appreciated what I had said. A very different reaction from the previous meeting a month before.

Carlos

It takes courage to be vulnerable. Some leaders erroneously assume it's a sign of weakness to admit you're wrong, but in fact it will often be viewed as a sign of strength. Gui's self-disclosure in that moment reduced the psychological distance between himself and the crowd. His admission and apology created a bridge that connected him to his audience.

A leader shows his strength by being humble enough to say, "I'm sorry—I made a mistake; forgive me."

Gui

The surprising outcome was that, afterward, people told me they wanted me to keep telling jokes! But I had already learned that telling jokes can be a dangerous way to run a meeting as you can unintentionally offend somebody. I could not run the risk of continuing to do this now that I represented this huge institution and so I had to find other ways to relax before addressing my team or 1,000 associates.

A Beautiful Commitment

Cristian Barrientos—Formerly COO of Walmex, Now CEO of Walmart Chile

I've had a long history with the company, 23 years in all. Before Gui came, the company was very disciplined and hierarchical. After he arrived as CEO, he broke the rules—in a good way! He has a relaxed style and loves to have fun, and he wanted the company to reflect that. Our traditional company began to evolve in unexpected ways.

At first, these changes were a shock for me. Some pushed back but most embraced this new culture of doing business. He instituted jeans day and a greater flexibility. We were less strict about meetings, and he encouraged those of us in the corporate office to have more of a connection with our 230,000 associates in the field. He eliminated the distance between the top level and middle management. But he also always made sure we were efficient with our time, which is essential for a retail operation. And we always had to deliver our targets.

I remember Gui telling me early on, "This company is like Disney. It's a big company, with lots of money, and lots of room to grow." He saw the opportunities that were here. One of the first things he did was to make sure all our stores had safe working conditions, sometimes installing new equipment. I saw it as a beautiful commitment to protect everyone in this company, and it came from his heart. That investment in safety meant a lot. He put his ideas into practice, and it showed me that people really mattered to him.

Gui

I believe you earn trust by being honest, reliable, and caring. These three qualities are fundamental. Another important aspect of building trust is to be an example to others. Fábio Barbosa, a CEO I admire, used to say a phrase that I have adopted in my life and career: "It works if you do the right thing the right way." A lot of times when you are in doubt about which option to choose, you are confronted with either "doing the right thing the right way" or taking a shortcut. My advice is to always go for the right thing the right way.

But caring deeply about people can sometimes get in the way of doing the right thing the right way. It took me years to understand this. Every time I analyzed my *past* performance in a certain job, I concluded that one of the things I could have done better was to make necessary changes to the team much sooner. I confused caring for people with protecting *or* subsidizing them, and on occasions I ended up hurting the very people I cared about.

This has been one of the most difficult things for me to learn and to change about myself. The first time I learned this lesson was at a very early stage in my career. I had been promoted to lead a department of four people, including me. My boss told me that due to restructuring I had to cut one person in the next few months and that he had already identified who the person should be. This person had more years working for the company than my age at that time. I believed that it was the company's fault that he was not performing. Why did they suddenly come to the conclusion, after 25 years, that this person was not good enough? Why hadn't he been given more help before this?

I tried to transfer him to another area, but nobody wanted him so I decided to keep him. After much deliberation I kept him in the same position and transferred the best employee I had (who many people wanted to hire) to another area to achieve the reduction in employees that I had been asked to do. I moved on to my next job feeling good about myself—I had *done the right thing*, not callously forcing a veteran of the company to find a new job.

After five years I returned to the same division of the same company but now in a much more senior position and, due to another restructuring, I was tasked again with firing him. At that stage, he was older and it was not easy for him to find a job on the outside. I realized if I had confronted the situation and made the difficult choice before, it would have been much better for this person. He would have at least been more employable than he was at the present time. By trying to be caring, I avoided a painful decision in the short term but it only led to making matters worse for him in the long term.

As we embarked on this massive transformation at Walmex, I had to keep in mind what had and hadn't worked for me in the past, but even that would no longer be enough. The future was full of unknowns and suddenly I couldn't simply count on making decisions that had helped me be successful before. I was committed to accomplishing my vision, but change always has a ripple effect, and I understood that those ripples didn't only have to do with technology but with people too. How would all of us, including me, be changed as we endeavored to turn this dream into a reality?

LEARNING POINTS FOR SUCCESSFUL LEADERS

Reinventing Yourself to Transform Your Company

Reinventing Yourself

- **Lesson:** Personal qualities such as competence, self-confidence, integrity, courage, and treating others with respect and dignity give the leader the necessary credibility to influence, to perform, and eventually to transform their organization.

> "Just as established products and brands need updating to stay alive and vibrant, you periodically need to refresh or reinvent yourself."
> —Mireille Guiliano

- **Lesson:** Don't confuse caring for people with tolerance for underperformance. Being a leader requires the appropriate and timely recognition that despite your efforts to help, someone may not want to change, adapt, or evolve . . . and that's when you must act swiftly.

> "Challenge yourself every day to do better and be better. Remember, growth starts with a decision to move beyond your present circumstances."
> —Robert Tew

Transform Your Company

- **Lesson:** To inspire others to follow, begin by shifting the mindset of leadership.

  "The world, as we have created it, is a process of our thinking. It cannot be changed without changing our thinking."
  —Albert Einstein

- **Lesson:** To help you make your customers' experience of your business easier and more enjoyable, utilize the best of what digital technology has to offer to genuinely get to know and understand them and their reality. Use agile methodology and data analytics to deliver the solutions more effectively and efficiently.

  "Until you understand your customers—deeply and genuinely—you cannot truly serve them."
  —Rasheed Ogunlaru

- **Lesson:** Good enough is good enough. Striving for perfection is an unreachable goal.

  "Don't aim for perfection. Aim for 'better than yesterday.'"
  —Izey Victoria Odiase

- **Lesson:** Go for the right thing the right way.

  "Do the work. Out-work. Out-think. Out-sell your expectations. There are no shortcuts."
  —Mark Cuban

The Key to Business Growth Is Self-Growth

4

"Progress is impossible without change, and those who
cannot change their minds cannot change anything."
—George Bernard Shaw

"To succeed in this world, you have to change all the time."
—Sam Walton, founder of Walmart

Gui

The mission was monumental: we had to overhaul the operations of our company—Walmart's biggest international market—learning new technologies while not jeopardizing the momentum we had recently achieved with the high performance of our past year. Since its initial founding, Walmex had been a customer-centric company, but our capacity to keep up that high standard had diminished in the digital era. By not maximizing our use of digital technologies, we weren't able to read our customers' needs and changing habits in the same data-driven way our digital-native competitors could. By not being agile, we weren't responding fast enough to our customers' requests. By not having an end-to-end organization, we weren't able to design and implement the right solutions with the speed and at the scale we desired. It would take a bold transformation to get the company where we needed it to be. As we faced instituting a tsunami of changes, we would have to keep delivering results without missing a single quarter of sales goals and without distracting our associates or disrupting service to our customers.

There were many mornings when, as I drove to work, I thought of the challenges ahead of me. I didn't find them daunting at this early stage; instead, my mind filled with the possibilities of what we could do. I felt as if I were on a journey without a map, and I wasn't even sure what my final destination would be.

But as I considered the myriad steps we needed to take to make the transformation successful, the one thing I didn't pay enough attention to—one that most leaders leave out of the equation—was how my own behavior needed to change. I needed to fall in love with the problem of my own emotional reactions and to listen more actively to my colleagues. We were talking every day about our customers' pain points, but I was forgetting about the pain points my team was experiencing because of me. This chapter reveals how I was forced to deal head-on with my own self-growth. There is no effective organizational transformation without effective personal reinvention of the leader.

The Challenge of Becoming Even More Customer-Centric

Before it was on my radar that I needed to change my own behavior, I was laser-focused on the changes my team would need to make as we redefined the operations of Walmex while preserving its familiar, iconic reputation. The transformation would impact every aspect of the company, and I knew there would be questions and even resistance for such an enormous overhaul, especially since we had just come off a year of exceptional sales.

People are generally reluctant to change and I knew this would be even more true at this time in 2017, when no one would see a pressing reason to. I could tell them we needed to become more competitive and customer-centric, but would they think I was undermining our recent victories by talking about possible defeat? It was clear to me that time wasn't on our side; I was thinking five years ahead and I was certain we'd be left in the dust unless we could begin to compete in a digital economy *now*.

I thought I could do what I'd always done before. Success gives a false impression that you have the magical formula and the only thing you have to do is to educate others about it so it gets repeated again and again. At least, that's what I thought at the time.

I hadn't yet come to appreciate that what had worked one year may not work at all the next. Consumers change, business environments change, employees change, so why should I be any different? But I hadn't grasped the fact that to implement all the changes I envisioned I would need to change too.

Despite years of experience and success, I believed that all I needed to do in order to transform the company was to bring the team along with me. That even though I wasn't sure about specifics I could share my enthusiasm and convey a general sense of what we could be, and then I was bound to get the kind of buy-in I needed. I felt I could speed up this process by inviting Carlos to help me align the team around my view of the transformation. He was both an old friend and one of the best leadership coaches I knew. I assumed that Carlos only needed to intervene with the team to make everything fine, as if they were the source of the problem.

I tried to force change, and it didn't work. At meetings I would speak passionately about what a transformation could mean for the company, but I was often met with bewildered looks and pushback. I got upset many times as I had the impression that people weren't listening to me or taking me seriously. When I spoke of leveraging technological advances, I heard people joke that I was coming up with futuristic fantasies that would doom the company. "What's next, Gui? Flying cars?" someone quipped.

In my conversations with Carlos, I began to realize that many times it wasn't about team members going against my ideas; it was more about me not being able to properly communicate what was on my mind. When I became emotional, I couldn't see that I was taking someone's resistance personally, and that obviously wasn't helpful. If people don't understand your idea, how can they contribute to improving it? I used to simply ignore those on my team that I felt weren't on "my side." I was behaving in contrast to how I needed to if I wanted to have people join me on this journey. They were asking for help, trying to understand what I meant by "the transformation," and yet I misread their questions as opposition and obstruction. When people disagreed with me, my reflex was to be dismissive and to cut them short before they could fully express their point of view. My passionate attitude for the mission was blinding me to the needs of the very people I'd need to help me fulfill it.

Montserrat Padierna, COE Lead Customer Knowledge & Experience, Walmex, and Gui's Chief of Staff for Two Years

In my experience, Gui has always been fair. And he had a vision of where he wanted to take Walmex. The sheer magnitude of the transformation of this legacy company was frightening for many, and some didn't think it was possible for Gui to accomplish all the changes he had in mind. At the beginning, he spoke of it as "his plan," "his strategy," and I remember telling him that if he wanted to bring people along with him, he needed to speak of it as "*our* plan," "*our* strategy." I know others were giving him the same advice. It was clear right from the start that many people felt shut out.

Because of the intense pressure he was under, Gui also became easily frustrated. I remember once I went into his office and I was critical of some new change he had proposed. We were always direct with each other, and I was often a sounding board for his ideas so I felt free to speak. He trusted me. That day I raised some points that may have been off-topic, and that distraction frustrated him. He had an outburst of anger but I understood what was behind it—that he was focused on delivering results, and when I brought up issues that weren't important it stressed him out. But he soon cooled down and apologized. I had become frustrated so I had to calm down too. He then explained what he needed from me and we came up with a plan of action that worked for both of us.

The Moment of Truth

Gui

The *premise* for the transformation was to bring Walmex into our modern technological age and help the business compete in a digital economy, but the *purpose* of the transformation was to become more customer-centric. As we were moving forward, we were also looking backward to honor the very roots of our company and our founder's vision. In the early stages of our journey, we didn't realize that our changes would be the first steps in building a whole-service ecosystem that was fully aligned with Sam Walton's vision to make life better for our customers.

The transformation was so complex that there were times I was moving at warp speed when the rest of the company was still trying to grasp which direction we were going. I'm passionate when I feel I have a purpose, and yet I didn't see that my exuberance was interfering with how I needed to lead my team through this period of unprecedented change and extreme stress.

Eduardo de la Garza, Chief Human Resources Officer, Walmex

I sat on the executive committee (Exco) with Gui's other direct reports, and at one meeting we felt we needed to discuss Gui's leadership style. He was there, and we asked him to step out for a while so we could talk frankly and then we would call him back in. He agreed. For 25 minutes we talked about how to give Gui feedback. Since I was head of HR, I was appointed to lead the conversation.

When Gui came back into the conference room he was very humble as he said to the group, "I want all of you to be willing to speak directly to me."

I told him that as his copilot and friend I would speak first, for just five minutes. That way he'd be able to digest the information. I could tell he was somewhat afraid as I started speaking. In clear terms I told him what we thought he was doing well but also things we didn't like. How he impatiently interrupted people when they were speaking if he thought he knew the answer. Or how he could sometimes be too direct, even rude, when someone disagreed with one of his decisions.

While I spoke, he took notes and paid close attention, his expression shifting from happy to upset. My five minutes stretched to fifteen. At the end of the meeting, Gui thanked us and left the room.

Gui

I was trying to understand what had caused my Exco team to feel the way they did so I asked Carlos for a coaching session. We went to a conference room where we could speak privately. There I informed him that I had listened attentively to the team's comments without interrupting; however, some of their observations did not seem correct to me.

"Look at all the notes they've given me," I said. "Do you think I'm as bad as they say I am?"

Carlos

I responded by suggesting that he didn't want to compound the situation by challenging or defending against what they said.

"Gui, it is not about how you or I perceive your behavior, but more importantly how they are perceiving it. This is the target to aim at. Besides, I've spoken to your team and there are many positive things they see in you as well as offering opportunities they believe you have to be even better. I believe I have a good idea of what is happening. What I heard on the negative side does not line up with the behaviors of the person I've known you to be. So again, I'll remind you: this is about behaviors you can correct, not an attack on who you are. Please separate these two realities."

Gui breathed a sigh of relief. "I knew you would help me prove the feedback was wrong and unfair."

I countered with, "I'm afraid that's not what I'm saying, Gui. People are 'seeing' you respond and behave in ways that neither support your leadership efforts for this company nor the transformation you are envisioning. In stressful situations you may be exhibiting certain behaviors that are undermining your leadership intentions. I'd like to help you process what was said so you can objectively understand how you are coming across to others."

I explained to Gui that he was being presented with an opportunity to improve and become an even more effective leader. I told him that it would take work for him to reframe how he was thinking about this feedback and to make the necessary changes but that I had faith in him. "I've seen you successfully tackle tough situations before, and I know you can meet this challenge now."

Luckily, because of my work with Gui in the past, he trusted me and was open to exploring what the issues were. I said, "First, people say you're not listening to them. Especially when you have the answer to a problem, you interrupt them and don't let them talk. So, members of your team assume a 'Why bother?' attitude, which is a convenient way of letting you make the decision and for them to just do as you say. If you truly want to transform the company, you need others to contribute, to feel respected, and to be engaged in coleading the transformation with you. Additionally, by not listening, you're not contributing to their development, to their willingness to participate and develop ownership in the process. Helping them be part of the change may be more important than you wanting to be right."

Gui

I knew immediately that Carlos was right, especially since it was not the first time I had been given this feedback. I was so focused on pushing my vision forward and getting it done as soon as possible that I didn't let others have their say. I could succeed without even noticing that I was damaging the capacity of the team to make their own decisions and succeed in future tasks.

Carlos

I needed to help Gui recognize the connection that existed between how he was *intellectually* processing the criticism he received and the *feelings* he was experiencing as a result. He needed to become aware of how these factors could possibly be triggering the kinds of behaviors others were noticing. It was essential for him to adopt the idea that his automatic, emotional responses did not need to be his default knee-jerk reactions. Gui had the option to make more effective behavioral choices and to work on consciously recognizing the situations that activated his negative reactions. As we began to unpack the process of making changes in himself, I said, "I want you to start by labeling everything you're feeling."

Gui

I told Carlos, "I feel betrayed, misunderstood, unappreciated, judged, angry, frustrated, and even afraid of possibly having failed my team."

Carlos

That was a good first step. I wanted Gui to understand that his feelings were most likely connected with his long-standing personal history of seeking perfection and approval. The intellectual process associated with how he was feeling was reflected in the doubts he was having as he asked me, "Do I fit in this organization? Am I being asked to be someone I'm not?"

Gui

The passion and enthusiasm that I brought to my position as CEO seemed to be in question, but they were the very qualities that had helped me be successful in the past. They were part of who I was. I valued being spontaneous and creative, and I couldn't stand rigidity and formalities.

Carlos

I emphasized that our work was not about changing "who he was." It was more about helping him recognize that there were "behavioral choices" he needed to manage more effectively, to remove the negative impact on what he was trying to accomplish.

The goals of my coaching work were threefold: to help Gui select and change the behaviors that were causing him problems, to gradually shift the perceptions his coworkers had of his behaviors, and to help him recognize and acknowledge the positive leadership qualities he brought to the table.

I asked Gui, "Are you ready to work on yourself? Do I have buy-in and commitment from you?"

Gui

I nodded and said, "Yes." Carlos was opening my eyes to something I had not thought about before—that the feedback I viewed as negative could really be a positive opportunity for me to change. I just had to get out of my own way to do the learning that was necessary. To grab the lifeline that he was throwing to me. He was helping me to understand that being dismissive or defensive about feedback from others was not going to be productive for my transformation or the company's.

Carlos

He knew this would not be an intellectual exercise but about getting in the trenches, rolling up his sleeves, and consistently following through in every one of his work-related interactions. I was encouraged, knowing that most of his coworkers were very supportive and willing to help him.

Empathic Silence: Learning to Listen

"The most important thing in communication is hearing what isn't said."
—Peter Drucker

Gui

When I became a CEO, I found that one of my main challenges as a leader was to learn that it was generally more important to ask the right questions than to have all the answers. As Carlos helped me understand, this requires active listening and accepting that others can have better answers than you.

I had to work hard on paying full attention to other people's opinions and to consider their point of view instead of impatiently providing a solution (even if my solution was a good one!). One message I received from the team was that even when I was listening, my body language gave the impression that I was not. Sometimes I would come back to a colleague and build on an idea that they had talked to me about days before and they were actually surprised—"You mean you actually *had* listened to what I said?" Perception is as important as reality.

Carlos

The feedback from the team had affected Gui deeply, and he sometimes wondered if attempting to get out from under this wave of perceived negativity was worth the effort. In some of our coaching conversations, I kept noticing that Gui would revert to interpreting the feedback as being about who he was personally and not about the consequences of how he was choosing to behave.

It's not easy for someone who's become accustomed to being a clever contributor in every conversation to realize that perhaps his most brilliant contribution may be "empathic silence," showing his collaborators that they are valued and truly being listened to. When he became frustrated, he'd justify his behavior by saying to me, "That's just the way I am," which tied the belief to his identity and how he defined himself, a way of thinking that, if not explored openly, would make the prospect of changing a difficult if not impossible proposition.

But Gui worked hard on being mindful of how others felt and responded to him, even reading between the lines of what they said to hear what their silences might reveal. This practice requires consistency and discipline so it becomes a natural part of our behavior. The more we demonstrate what we have learned, the more we reinforce it and the more habitual it becomes.

As we made progress and Gui gained confidence and clarity over several sessions, I advised him to share with his Exco his development opportunities and work. I believed that they would see it as a sign of strength that he was willing to make changes in himself as he inspired his team to partner with him in changing the company.

Gui

I understood what Carlos wanted me to do, but I was struggling to figure out how I would be able to make people believe that my intentions were sincere and that they would see me make real progress. I asked Carlos, "How will I bring them to my side and convince them to help me more with the company transformation?"

Carlos

I responded, "I know you may think some of them may be skeptical of your intentions and some may doubt how committed you are to changing your behavior. But remember the old adage 'actions speak louder than words.' How you respond to their feedback over time will be more effective than anything you tell them now. Tell them about the three key areas that are the focus of your change efforts and share the results you plan to deliver in those areas. Keep in mind, it's best to underpromise and overdeliver. Eventually, your actions and the consistency of your follow-up will reassure them that you are serious about making changes.

"Also, it will be very helpful for you to make a clear distinction between 'the essence of who you are as a person' and 'the behaviors you have chosen to improve based on feedback you've received.' When people offer you their feedback, don't assume they are judging you—but rather that they're providing you with their views on how you as their leader can help them do better.

"The fact that some will be skeptical is related to how they have experienced you up to this point and is only normal behavior. It's your job to change their opinion by showing them you're making real efforts to make changes and grow."

Gui

I agreed to share with the Exco the improvement plan that Carlos and I had drafted, but I must confess I only did so because he told me it was a necessary part of the coaching process.

I decided to be very transparent about what I needed to work on in myself. This would be my test. At the next Exco meeting, two weeks after the one where my team had spoken to me about my behavior, I looked at everyone who sat around the conference table. These were my colleagues, my friends, and I wanted to be worthy of their trust in me. They didn't have a clue as to what I was about to share and, at that moment, I knew I had to let my heart do the talking.

I began by saying, "I want to thank you all for the feedback you gave me and for taking the time to talk to Carlos too. I want you to know that I am grateful. He and I went over the notes I took at the last meeting—about the good qualities you see in me as well as where I need to improve. I am profoundly serious about changing and taking the opportunities I have to do better and improve as a leader.

"First, I would like to apologize for having misbehaved. Based on the way I've behaved, scaring some people by talking at every forum about the transformation without being clear and not listening closely enough to what you had to say, I really want to change and improve. I would like to ask you to help me as I move forward. It is important for me to let my actions and not just my words reflect my sincerity about making the changes I need to make. I promise you I will work hard to succeed.

"Based on your feedback and my work with Carlos, I have selected three main target areas to work on:

- To be a more effective and patient listener.
- To remain calm and collected when things don't go as I expected.
- And to be more attentive and thoughtful about what I say and to whom I say it.

"If you agree that these are important issues for me to work on, you can help me by providing recommendations and suggestions for me to consider. Trust that I'll try hard to change. Please be aware that there may be times when

I may fall back to my old behaviors, and I'm asking you to please help me see it when it happens. I promise I'll listen to you and be grateful."

When I finished speaking, I could tell from the expressions on their faces that they were surprised I had an improvement plan and had asked them for help. They smiled and nodded their support, and the warmth of their reaction gave me the stimulus I needed to change.

Carlos

I liked that Gui asked them to help him to change. Inviting them to support his efforts would give him another opportunity to lead by example, generate cooperation, and hopefully inspire his team to initiate their own improvement journeys. I wished he had also acknowledged the positive qualities they saw in his leadership, too, and I tried to help him not lose sight of this fact.

Gui

The gracious encouragement I received from my team took a huge weight off my shoulders and made me feel better. I was able to work on how I listened to others, and I learned to wait before responding to an idea that I didn't agree with.

Montserrat Padierna, COE Lead Customer Knowledge & Experience, Walmex, and Gui's Chief of Staff for Two Years

As Gui worked on his own behavior, I saw him begin to take time to think through what he was going to say, to withhold reacting instead of getting frustrated right away. He truly learned to *listen*.

The thing about Gui is that, unlike any other leader I've worked with, he is a CEO who gives fully of himself. He's an open-door CEO who loves to ask questions and gather information from many different "thermometers"—not only his direct reports but people at our stores and suppliers too. When he believes he's been wrong, he apologizes, and he turns it into a way for him *to learn*—wanting to know how he can be more effective in getting the mission done, and in those early years that meant the massive work of transforming the company. It's his humility and desire to do better that separates him from other leaders who feel they always know best.

Progress, Not "Perfection"

Gui

One of the major goals of the transformation was to be fully responsive to the needs of our consumers. To do this, we would have to become more flexible, making changes in our operations as we detected shifts in buying habits. In addition, we needed to bring new products to market with more speed; rather than taking time to develop a full concept and extensively test it before introducing it to our customers, we began to concentrate on creating MVPs (Minimum Viable Products), testing them with initial users, and improving or discarding them based on their feedback. Instead of spending a lot of time to develop a "perfect" product, our approach was to rethink the process and launch a "good enough" product that was better than previous versions or the competition. We could refine it as we received input from our customers on what they felt could make it better. The key was not to try to resolve every issue all at once but to focus on adjusting just a few things with each iteration of the product.

I told my team, "Let's keep in mind we all grew up trying to be perfect so let's not be too hard on ourselves when we do mess up." I wasn't prepared for how my words would end up coming back to haunt me. Suddenly, when people made big mistakes, they refused feedback on how to improve, using the excuse that I had told them to make more mistakes. I had difficulty dealing with this until I learned that we were taking the wrong approach: we were *celebrating our mistakes* when we should have been *celebrating what we learned from them* instead.

A learning organization transforms mistakes into lessons. We kept improving by applying those lessons to transform weaknesses into strengths. Great leaders do the same thing. To work this way, we had to be able to have difficult conversations, accept feedback with an open mind, and leave behind any solutions that we fell in love with but our customers did not. It required a change, not only in the way we did things but the way we *thought about* what we were doing.

Just as my team needed to listen to consumer feedback on our MVPs, I had to keep paying attention to what my colleagues were saying to me about my own behavior. I was far from "perfect," but I could improve, and if I tried to work on a few issues instead of trying to resolve all of them at once, I would be better than I was before.

Carlos

Gui and I had several conversations about the idea that, rather than striving for perfection by avoiding mistakes and aiming for flawless execution, the emphasis needed to be placed on promoting constant learning, exploration, and growth. I was very pleased with how he incorporated these concepts, drawing from his experiences, to help himself and influence his team members.

Rethinking Titles

Gui

We knew we wanted to change the hierarchical nature of our company, breaking down the silos that separated departments, and building a new unity and agility that would ultimately be reinforced by the formation of our multidisciplinary teams.

One of our most radical changes, especially for a company as traditional as Walmex, was for us to do away with standard titles, which often reinforced the ego-driven nature of most businesses. Suddenly, this aspect of each person's business identity was reinvented: vice presidents became "tribe leads," directors became "squad leads." It was strange for people at first, disorienting, as Alejandra Paczka discovered. She decided to leave her job at a digital company to join our transformation team at Walmex because she felt our purpose and values aligned with her own. She not only brought her digital expertise to the company but her ability to persuade people to buy in to change.

Alejandra Paczka, Chief Talent Officer, Walmex

Gui wanted to break down the symbols of our corporate culture, the walls that literally and figuratively separated us. We changed the way of working and the organizational structure. When it came to titles, we started from scratch, trying to be innovative and creative. Initially it shook some people up. As I spoke about how everyone would be given a new descriptive title, one team member looked upset as he raised his hand. "You mean I won't be a VP anymore?"

"That's right," I said. "From now on you will be a tribe lead. But your salary will not change, don't worry."

Gui

People began to embrace the creative descriptions of their new titles that signaled a different way of identifying what they did. If we were going to transform our operations, we also needed to radically rethink every aspect of our business, from the titles we used to the way we shared information to the office spaces where we worked.

We were wasting a great deal of energy due to the lack of synchronization caused by silos. Over time we would develop 24 multidisciplinary teams working to identify the end-to-end pain points our customers and associates were feeling, often due to the old ways we had operated the business. Because people from different departments were speaking to one another instead of being separated by silos, they were able to implement solutions in a more agile way.

Suddenly, many of our employees wanted to join one of these teams. They saw that agile teams were producing better results with more frequency and were happier than their coworkers in other areas.

At the beginning, the new pilot teams were crowded in very small rooms. We decided to renovate part of the office space to accommodate our vision of building multidisciplinary teams working together; walls were knocked down to create more open space, with long tables that were cool and modern. The day we inaugurated the offices, we felt they represented the spirit of what we wanted to achieve: a new freedom to exchange ideas and come up with solutions. We called the new space Zone 18—*18* because the project was achieving maturity (and also because it was 2018) and *Zone* referred to the sports phrase of being "in the zone," when an athlete is on a roll, mentally and physically, bringing their A-game to everything they do.

From a Leader of Internal Support Services, Walmex

As someone who often has confidential discussions on complex matters with people in the company, I was firmly opposed to giving up my private office. I had a discussion with Gui to let him know how I felt, since I knew I could be direct with him. He listened and responded, "We have to have everybody be all in on this with no exceptions. I'm giving up my private office too. Everyone has to see that we are not the same hierarchical company we were before. Communication has to be more open, and doing away with walls will symbolize that. Think it over and let me know your decision." It was a change I wasn't comfortable with, but Gui presented me with reasons that went beyond me or any one individual. I believed in supporting the transformation, so after giving it considered thought, I let Gui know I was all in with his vision.

Competitor Intel

Gui

One of the prime reasons for the transformation was to become competitive with digitally native start-ups that had grown increasingly successful in the past 10 years. They had become adept at connecting with customers, providing ease of ordering, and capturing market share through compelling brand-storytelling. Despite our previous, highly profitable year, I saw that these threats were not hovering in the future, but were a present danger, especially in the United States and Asia. If we didn't act quickly, the leverage we had would be lost. In order to understand our competitive advantages and disadvantages, we needed to gather intelligence on what other companies were doing to move ahead. I relied on a technique I had used effectively for many years in the past: running strategic war games.

At Unilever we would assemble a group of our employees from various areas and backgrounds and split them into teams. One team would represent our company and the other teams would play the role of our competitors as we'd simulate different scenarios (such as a product launch) to game out various outcomes. This kind of competitive intelligence helped us to think more tactically about gaining an edge over other companies. At one point, we were able to visit with the Royal Marines based in the United Kingdom to discuss war games with them. It was a thrilling day for me—to learn how similar our processes were, and to hear these experienced officers tell us they were impressed by our strategies.

As I geared up for Walmex to make its transformation, I gathered my team members together to engage in such similar competitive intelligence: we needed to strategize how we, a brick-and-mortar retail business, could get ahead of emerging, digitally native businesses. Could we use our advantages (physical stores, scale, trust) to rise above our competitors who were causing such disruptions in the marketplace? Working in silos, as we were used to, would not have provided us with the answer. But the shift to multidisciplinary teams would open up our thinking and help us anticipate what others were doing so we could develop new opportunities to surpass them.

Difficult Choices

Gui

A transformation of this kind requires a company-wide commitment. Nobody can do it alone. As a leader, you need to recruit people who share your idea that the company must change to continue to prosper. Some of them can come from the inside and others will inevitably need to be hired from the outside. In the case of our transformation, we hired many people who were eager to join us as they saw this as an opportunity to have a bigger impact than if they stayed at the companies where they were, even though they had top positions there and loved their work. A number of them had been CEOs and leaders in their companies, some with decades of experience, but they saw becoming part of our team as a once-in-a-lifetime chance to make a difference in the lives of others.

Though we kept a majority of our employees, our Exco was made up of 50% new hires with impressive leadership backgrounds. For example, Eduardo de la Garza, our Chief Human Resources Officer, had been at PepsiCo for 32 years; Alejandra Paczka, our Chief Talent Officer, had been with Microsoft for 8 years, most recently as their CHRO; and Beatriz ("Betty") Núñez had been with Terra Networks Telefonica for 22 years. When we met with Betty, she was their CEO, responsible for 19 countries. I told her that we didn't have a defined position to offer her, but I wanted her to be part of the company. What convinced such successful leaders to sign on?

I started my conversations with them by talking about scale: Walmex has 6,000 associates in our headquarters and more than 230,000 working in our stores. The fact that our company touches the lives of so many employees and customers helped me to make a persuasive case for high-level leaders to join us. They came on board with fresh ideas and no attachment to Walmex's past. Most importantly, they had a desire to do whatever it took to deliver the vision that we knew was possible for the future. They suffered a lot of resistance from their teams and colleagues at the beginning; their style was different and there were some among our old guard who tried to force them out. But their years of experience as leaders in other companies had given them a sense of determination and resilience. They had a great desire to make things happen, and I made sure to support them so we could implement the bold changes we needed to make.

I began to learn that it was more difficult to identify those who were opposed to the transformation. They were unwilling to tell me what they were really thinking, and so I tried to put my energy into finding people in the company who were openly in favor of the plans I proposed. I spent time with them, listening to their innovative ideas.

Carlos

By its very nature, the concept of transformation is disruptive and often brings about an unintended conflict between those with experience in what helped the company be successful in the past and those with knowledge of recent technologies and methods that could help the business succeed in the future. The manifestations of this conflict are not always overt but may simmer below the surface, a combination of resentments and fears that people try to hide as they endeavor to make sense of what is happening and to figure out how these changes will benefit them.

Three group behavioral descriptions have been outlined in the literature by various researchers regarding how individuals react when facing changes in their organizational environments: contributors, passive observers, and detractors.

Contributors: These individuals are quick to get on board. Despite the constant changes, they can concentrate on numerous new opportunities to learn and participate in something they view as positive, meaningful, and motivating. They are eager to get involved and will be valuable team members who will enthusiastically demonstrate their commitment to supporting and facilitating the changes necessary for the transformation to progress.

Passive Observers: This group is described as cautious, choosing to sit on the sidelines and observe how things are progressing. Some believe they can wait for this new management trend to pass. Change leaders must proactively reach out, listen to their concerns, and address them in order to engage and bring them on board.

Detractors: This is the most challenging group. These individuals reveal themselves with varying degrees of intensity—some show their feelings more overtly, and others more covertly, creating stealth opposition. Some may feel justified in defending their entrenched position, while others may be threatened by the changes they see coming. I've seen situations where some even agree to the proposed change without having any real intention of bringing it about. They often have difficulty expressing points of view that they perceive as unpopular or that may put them in conflict with those in charge.

Each group has its own motives. At first, Gui chose to work with the contributors, but he soon needed to engage and recruit those who sat on the fence.

Detractors require special attention. It is important to actively listen and try to understand their concerns rather than judging them as problems based on previous history and experiences. Their fears and points of view may be related to their professional background and the beliefs they have adopted, which are supported by the organizational culture they are a part of.

As Gui brought his team together, we agreed that his key message to them had to be: "The transformation train has already left the station. Let's all work together and help each other to make the journey a success."

Gui

After we piloted the new way of working and were about to promote the change in the organization, I heard rumors that there were detractors who were telling people that this major change was never going to happen. So I called a meeting with our whole team in the auditorium and I spoke plainly to them. "This transformation will happen. I would be happy to help anyone who is against it to leave. You will receive a generous severance if you feel someplace else will suit you better."

This approach was a necessary jolt. We didn't have a moment to lose and I needed to make sure I had a team that would be fully committed. No exceptions, no excuses. As usual, there were those who loved that I was so direct, while others were shocked. But after that meeting everyone was certain about my intention. They knew from working with me that when I say something will happen, I make it happen.

The Follow-Up Factor

Carlos

As the transformation of the company gained momentum, Gui and I continued our coaching sessions. When we spoke about his own journey of growth, I emphasized, "A plan is just a plan unless it is put into action. Perhaps the most important part of the process is the quality and consistency of the follow-up."

I encouraged Gui to continue checking in with his stakeholders to ask them how he was doing so he could fine-tune his own progress. In their comprehensive study "Leadership Is a Contact Sport: The 'Follow-Up Factor' in Management Development," Dr. Marshall Goldsmith and Howard Morgan surveyed 11,480 business leaders on four continents and concluded that those who made repeated efforts to follow up on their action plans measurably improved their effectiveness. I knew that for Gui to succeed in his personal action plan, he needed to demonstrate his commitment to improving as he promised by following up with individual members of his team and the Exco as a whole, and doing it consistently.

Gui

When I did follow up, sometimes I received very different views about my behavior, which was confusing. For example, during a meeting about an issue I cared deeply about, the team expressed a number of contrary views. I responded directly about why I felt we needed to take a particular course of action. The team seemed to still be in doubt and I was concerned that they weren't going to reach a consensus, so I imposed my point of view, making an executive decision. After the meeting, I heard two different kinds of opinions. Some told me that I had misbehaved like in the past—that I had not listened enough and was "too bossy." Meanwhile, others congratulated me for being "firm and decisive." For a long time, I used the positive feedback from that meeting and others to justify my old behavior and avoid changing.

Carlos

This is a situation where I cautioned Gui not to get seduced by the feedback that made him feel good because it tolerated his own "misbehavior."

"Gui," I said, "there will always be some who will have no problem if you are 'too bossy.' However, in this case, there were others in the room who did not feel heard, and this was something you told them you would be working on. But a decision needed to be made, and that is what you focused on. As we have discussed, it is relevant for them to understand that once everyone's opinion has been heard and considered, then a decision must be made. Even if there is no consensus, the whole team must agree to support it going forward.

"I believe you will need to distinguish 'the what' from 'the how'—making the decision for the group in that meeting was 'the what,' and the way you did it was 'the how.' But there's also the 'why' factor. Ask the team members who felt excluded if they understood *why* you felt compelled to make a unilateral decision. It's imperative to have this difficult conversation, to circle back with them to check out how it impacted them."

Gui

I understood what Carlos was saying and, in that situation, I have to say I was very happy with the positive feedback.

Carlos

It was natural for Gui to appreciate the affirming response. "All leaders do," I said. "The fact that you have a team that thinks diversely is good and should be valued. But you must keep in mind that when there are conflicting points of view about your leadership approach, you need to use it as an opportunity to generate cohesion and cooperation, and not to justify engaging in behaviors that you said were going to change."

Gui

Another important insight that came up in my coaching sessions with Carlos was that changing my behavior was one thing but changing other people's *perceptions* of that behavior was another. I believed I was changing, but people weren't fully recognizing it.

Carlos

I let Gui know that based on my and many of my colleagues' experiences with other leaders who changed their behaviors, it took their teams a bit longer than they anticipated to recognize there had been a shift. Their colleagues needed time to revise their long-held perceptions and to catch up with the way their CEOs were evolving.

I said, "Gui, perceptions others have of you will not always keep pace with the incremental changes you're making. But I assure you that if your new behaviors consistently demonstrate that you are making progress and that you are enlisting their help and support, it will favorably impact how they see you."

Gui

There was another problem that resulted from my telling everyone I needed their help as I made changes. People took my invitation to offer feedback so seriously that I started to receive a steady stream of suggestions on a daily basis. It was like an overdose of feedback.

People were telling me what they wanted me to be—but it was based on their own idea of what a CEO should be, rather than on who I was. They were even correcting specific words I had used and giving me their suggestions for other words I should use instead. It was so overwhelming that I stopped listening.

Carlos

People had good intentions, but they often felt they had free license to walk into Gui's office and douse him with whatever suggestions they felt he needed to hear. This was upsetting and uncomfortable for Gui because people weren't respecting boundaries and often seemed more interested in what they wanted from him rather than what he needed from them.

This was a delicate process that required calibration because Gui didn't want to be perceived as rejecting the very feedback he had asked for. That would have defeated his intent to reach out for help in the first place. I suggested that Gui could acknowledge their efforts and show appreciation for their input, and also emphasize that they could be more helpful to him if they stayed exclusively focused on the three issues he was working on instead of on a wide variety of additional areas.

Gui

Finally, I managed to tell them that the excess of feedback was making me feel less self-confident and that it would be more helpful if their feedback and suggestions stayed focused on the issues I was working on. Once my team understood this, things began to improve.

It takes time and consistent effort to change, and this was a long and lonely journey. But it was ultimately worth it as I saw myself becoming a better colleague and a better boss, and it improved my chances of being successful with the company's transformation. The Listening Checklist that follows could serve as a useful template for any leader who wants to improve in this critical skill:

- Are my team members coming to me with their concerns or going to others?
- Am I able to listen to others without interrupting them?

- Can I put my ego aside when listening to critical feedback?
- Do I remain calm, mindful, and receptive when someone doesn't agree with me?
- Am I aware of my body language when interacting with others?

The Next Step in the Journey

Gui

The most difficult part of my learning process—and probably a key pivot point for me—was when I had to tell my team about my desire to improve my behavior and ask them for their help. I had been upset by some of the feedback and suspicious about whom I could trust. I managed to bring my emotions under control when I talked with them, but it took me a long time to realize why others didn't often criticize me directly; it was because *I wasn't making it easy for them*. I had to learn to trust their motives, to believe they *wanted* me to succeed.

As we discussed in chapter 1, Simon Sinek, in *The Infinite Game*, defines the title phrase as a game that's not about winning but keeping the game going, breaking conventions, and creating businesses that are "strong enough and healthy enough to stay in the game for many generations to come." As Sinek writes, "When leaders are willing to prioritize trust over performance, performance always follows." By trusting the people to help me during the improvement process, I was also increasing their involvement and trust in me.

Carlos was telling me that follow-up conversations with my team were an important part of the process; I would need to find out from them how I was doing. It was coming up on six months from the meeting when I made promises to improve. Now I would surprise them (and myself) by asking for a "performance review" at the next Exco meeting. Would I be up to asking for a candid assessment? And if I was, would I be able to handle hearing their feedback? I would soon find out.

LEARNING POINTS FOR SUCCESSFUL LEADERS

Reinventing Yourself to Transform Your Company

Reinventing Yourself

- **Lesson:** Doing the hard, personal work it takes to get to know yourself better is fundamental to growing and maturing as a leader. It requires having the humbleness and curiosity of a novice, which will allow you to have new insights and flourish free of the sanctions of your own self-perceptions.

> "Great leaders encourage leadership development
> by openly developing themselves."
> —Dr. Marshall Goldsmith

- **Lesson:** Leadership coaching is about actively learning more about yourself, to further develop your strengths and the capacity to learn from your weaknesses as well.

> "You get the best effort from others not by lighting a
> fire beneath them, but by building a fire within."
> —Bob Nelson

- **Lesson:** One of the best ways for you to value and show others the respect they need and deserve is to genuinely listen to them.

> "A real conversation always contains an invitation. You
> are inviting another person to reveal herself or himself
> to you, to tell you who they are or what they want."
> —David Whyte

Transform Your Company

- **Lesson:** Connecting the transformation process to a transcendental and meaningful purpose provides you and others with a compelling reason to change.

  > "No man or woman is an island. To exist just for
  > yourself is meaningless. You can achieve the most
  > satisfaction when you feel related to some greater
  > purpose in life, something greater than yourself."
  > —Denis Waitley

- **Lesson:** It's vital for you to provide clarity of vision so that everyone is on board and aligned with it. Communicate, communicate, and communicate the vision . . . it is never too much.

  > "No matter what business you're in, everyone
  > in the organization needs to know why."
  > —Frances Hesselbein

- **Lesson:** A transformation requires replacing current organizational thinking with more upgraded models. The attitude of "We've always done it this way" can be extremely costly.

  > "And the day came when the risk to remain tight in a
  > bud was more painful than the risk it took to blossom."
  > —Anaïs Nin

- **Lesson:** Resiliency and adaptability are two important catalysts that will help you generate opportunities for the company.

  > "Resiliency is the ability to spring back from
  > and successfully adapt to adversity."
  > —Nan Henderson

- **Lesson:** Value the leadership talent of your team and invest in the continued growth and development of those who are able and willing to cope with change as the company evolves.

> "One of the greatest talents of all is the talent
> to recognize and develop talent in others."
> —Colin Powell

- **Lesson:** Transforming the company's way of working comes with risks, but playing it safe in a rapidly changing context is not an option. Being able to deliver your targets will always provide you with more latitude to change.

> "Determination, energy, and courage appear spontaneously
> when we care deeply about something. We take
> risks that are unimaginable in any other context."
> —Margaret J. Wheatley

5

360-Degree Learning

"In learning, you will teach, and in teaching, you will learn."
—Phil Collins

Gui

One of the challenges we faced at the beginning of our transformation was that most of the senior managers of Walmex were not proficient users of technology and had never worked for digital-native companies. Entering the world of digital technology was like visiting a foreign country where they didn't speak the language, and many on our leadership team did not fully grasp the possibilities of a technology that wasn't familiar to them. We started to talk about moving toward e-commerce without having the minimum digital skills—even to do basic tasks—in our personal lives.

It's not a surprise that the young people working for us liked the idea of utilizing technology but were a little bit suspicious of leadership's capacity to do it. And investors and analysts were also skeptical, with some saying we should continue managing our physical stores and leave e-commerce to those digital-native companies who were already fully equipped to handle it. A number of financiers felt they'd rather diversify their investments by becoming shareholders in digital companies where technology was part of their DNA.

But from the beginning we saw this transformation as a crucial move toward a successful future. We understood that the experience and scale in physical retail could become a competitive advantage in the digital world. Our customers would start to buy online, but they would also continue to shop at our physical stores. We had to become an omnichannel company to be able to serve them in whatever ways they wanted. Their needs had evolved, and our business had to evolve to keep providing the kind of effective service they expected from us.

This chapter is all about 360-degree learning, the many different ways available to us at Walmex to evolve, adapt, and grow, from working with a professional coach with wide-ranging executive expertise helping business leaders, to my senior team receiving mentoring from a younger generation who grew up with a digital mindset. My job was to encourage everyone to draw on the best from all sources and to be open to learning. To make sure they understood the importance of wisdom that comes from years of experience and to respect the value of fresh knowledge that comes from a deep understanding of current technology. Past experience alone is not enough, and neither is fresh knowledge. It's about taking advantage of help that can come from all directions. That also means taking courses and attending conferences, reading articles, visiting other companies, and talking to experts in the field. There is so much knowledge available to us—we just have to be willing to seek it out.

If our aim was to become a leading omnichannel company, we needed to make sure our team included both experienced brick-and-mortar retailers as well as digital associates. But how to make this combination a winning formula?

When we began discussing the idea of transformation, some of our more digitally savvy associates approached me and we engaged in extensive conversations about where to take the company. They saw in my willingness to transform the company a terrific opportunity for them to apply their knowledge to this massive project. It would give them the chance to thrive doing what they loved to do, and they embraced it wholeheartedly.

Such forward-thinking executives in our company as Lety Espinosa, Carlos da Silva, Philip Bhen, and many others were part of a group of people who formulated the first steps of our transformation. It became clear to us that we would have to train our people and that it should start with our executive committee. Working with a consulting company, Philip organized a trip to San Francisco where we attended lectures about digital technology and agile methodology and their impact on retail. Like my earlier visit to Singularity University in Santa Clara, it was an illuminating trip that taught us more about the possibilities of technology and how it could be applied to a diverse range of businesses. We also visited a mix of digital-native companies as well as more traditional ones that were also going through their own transformations.

Since learning is a passion of mine, I loved immersing myself in this process. My team and I attended a number of events, like the South by Southwest conference in Austin, Texas (mentioned in chapter 3), where speakers and panelists provided us with practical strategies. At the beginning I felt quite ignorant, but with the help of my younger colleagues I started to gain a deeper understanding of technology and to feel more comfortable talking about it. Instead of speaking about transformation in such vague terms that others felt confused, I started to pinpoint actual techniques we could utilize. My coach, Carlos, had emphasized the importance of clear communication, and I was beginning to grasp how essential it was to back up my enthusiasm with specifics.

Also, the fact that other Walmart companies around the world were going through the same experiences to become digitally proficient meant that we could reach out to one another for support. Because we have a culture of sharing, we were able to exchange thoughts about what was working and what wasn't, which accelerated our learning.

Of course, sometimes I felt like my younger colleagues were speaking a foreign language, and it took me time to fully understand certain concepts. Luckily, they were patient with me. I admit I was embarrassed and some of my colleagues were, too, when we were asked if we were using certain digital tools such as Facebook and Instagram, among others. It didn't help for us to ask our kids to teach us since they would do the task so fast that we still didn't understand how to do it on our own.

Reverse Mentoring

Gui

As I read about how businesses managed transformations and talked to experts, a consulting company presented me with data from 2016, which indicated that companies going through similar digital-agile transformations as ours usually retired about 50 percent of their head offices and hired 30 percent new associates. But none of them were even close to our size. Walmex had 6,000 associates at its head office, and I was resolute about keeping as many of my team intact as possible, but with one caveat: everyone (including me!) would have to agree to be trained in the new technology we'd need to use.

Somebody at our company had the idea of allocating a young, digitally proficient associate to each senior manager so they could patiently help us to use digital tools. We referred to that as "reverse mentoring." The younger associates were tremendously helpful in giving us guidance as we began to experiment in the digital world, and at the same time, they benefited from listening to the opinions of their more experienced managers, who could help them learn about the business.

There was some friction, and I found myself needing to intervene when our successful veteran team members didn't see the need to change and certainly didn't want to be coached on how to become more digitally literate by new hires half their age.

Fortunately, the experience was ultimately successful and influenced our decision not to replace a huge number of senior managers. While a different solution may have helped us advance quickly and achieve our technological goals, we had to think about what we would lose in terms of the combined wisdom that our senior managers bring to other aspects of running our retail business. By having a system of reverse mentoring, we could hold onto our best longtime managers by having them be trained by our up-and-coming associates, who would in turn benefit from their older mentees' years of experience.

In my case, Montserrat ("Montse") Padierna became my digital mentor (and later she would become my chief of staff). She was very patient with me, teaching me how to use technology and explaining the logic of it as well (yes, I wanted to know *how* it worked as well as how to use it). Montse even gave me a gift in teaching me to use voice assistant. On the other hand, she learned to become more patient with the pace of change our company could take. For a long time she kept saying we were going too slow without fully understanding all the dimensions of changing a company of our size. We both learned from each other and we both became better leaders.

Montserrat ("Montse") Padierna, COE Lead Customer Knowledge & Experience, Walmex, and Gui's Chief of Staff for Two Years

I was first told about Walmex by a manager I used to work for who said the company was doing things differently. I was very curious and took a chance on working there, starting in e-commerce as part of the network team. The company wanted to become more digital, and they asked us to sign up if we were interested in mentoring others in that area, helping them learn about such social networking sites as Twitter and Facebook. My background was in marketing and social media, so I submitted my name and randomly I was assigned to mentor Gui.

It was funny at the beginning. I had just started at the company and suddenly I am having monthly meetings with the CEO to teach him about all things digital! Gui was always so open-minded, so humble. He told me, "I don't know a lot about this, but I'm curious. I want to understand, so please be patient with me." We did small projects at first, like opening a Twitter account for him and establishing a strategic presence for him online with a LinkedIn profile. These things helped him understand, bit by bit, at his own pace and in his own language, what digital was all about.

Each session was one hour. I would come to his office and see him reading and analyzing material about technology. He said, "I don't know anything about this—can you teach me?" He not only posed questions but asked for feedback about how he was doing. That startled me. I wasn't used to having these kinds of straightforward, even vulnerable conversations with the leader of a company.

We may have started with simple things, like helping him learn about Twitter, but I saw how he was connecting it to bigger ideas, and his thinking evolved over time. He was a different type of leader. I had never worked with anyone like him before in my career.

Gui

It was a major task to recruit digital-native people to join us. In the beginning, we even had difficulty reaching them. They would not always return our calls and the ones who did usually just wanted to know what a company as important as Walmart was calling them about.

We ultimately found the right way to persuade potential candidates to come work with us. The pitch that was most effective was the simple truth: we asked them to consider the company's purpose, which was to help our customers live better, and our scale would allow these candidates to have a much bigger impact on more people than the job they currently had. Walmex's mission resonated with them and was often the deciding factor.

Creating the Possibility for Change Agents to Be Creative

Gui

As our internal discussions about the transformation became more frequent and filtered to the outside world and our mother company was moving fast in its own efforts, it helped us to attract people. In previous chapters, you've heard directly from Betty Núñez, Eduardo de la Garza, and Ale Paczka, three outstanding hires who were already top leaders at their previous companies. Each one was instrumental in moving the transformation forward and impacting the lives of our associates as well as our customers. The same was true of Ignacio Caride, who agreed to come to Walmex from Mercado Libre, even though he had a competing offer. He was a crucial associate, bringing his wealth of experience with digital-native companies to help us in our journey from brick-and-mortar retailer to agile, omnichannel company. Once these notable achievers joined Walmex, it became easier to recruit others, who brought their technological expertise to our efforts and helped us realize our vision of becoming fully digital so that we could meet our customers' needs.

However, life at work was not always easy for them, especially in those early years. Their way of working was different—they were risk-takers, much more than many in the company, but they believed in taking calculated risks, and they were used to having data available instantaneously to help in decision-making processes. They were also more ambitious about sales growth than many others at the company, and even though we had a culture of being "good implementers," they wanted to see things happen at a speed that was much faster than what we had been used to. Several of our longtime associates started to get scared and to criticize the "newcomers." We had to find a way to accommodate both groups and alleviate any potential tension. The new associates had capabilities we did not, and they were unfamiliar with the rules that our veteran team members valued.

One of my high-level executives who had been with the company for years and done impressive work asked to meet with me. After taking a seat in my office, they immediately brought up their concerns, naming a new hire who had been given a leadership role.

"Gui, the way that person is conducting business is quite different from the way we do things, and it scares me."

I replied, "I understand, but the reason we hired this person is exactly *because* they do things differently."

"Well, I've alerted you several times to my concerns, and I don't think you're taking them seriously enough."

"I'm sorry you feel that way," I said, choosing my words carefully as Carlos had helped me to do. "Let me share my concern: I'm worried about how to move toward the strategic direction we've set for our company. So let me ask you, do you agree with our company's need to change, to become digital?"

The executive nodded and spoke resolutely. "I fully agree with the strategy and am all in."

"Okay, let's just imagine that I fire this person and replace them with you. Or I try to do their job. Do you think we can succeed?"

The executive looked surprised and quickly said, "No, I think we'd certainly fail as we don't have the capabilities and digital experience they bring to our company."

"Well, then," I replied, "we need to change our perspective! Instead of criticizing, we need to help those new associates adapt to our rules without losing their capacity to implement new ways of doing things. It's up to us to welcome them and help them understand how to follow certain rules that will not change."

"Got it," the executive said, standing up. "Okay! You can count on me."

This type of conversation occurred many times in my office, with many different leaders, and the conclusion was always the same. Company veterans would warn me about the danger of adding new associates to the team; they were fearful that these new hires were taking actions that disrupted the status quo. My response was that the status quo needed to change and we needed these leaders because they had important capabilities we did not have.

Carlos

The role of the leader in this case is to stop attacks, to defend and protect their transformational contributors. The warnings from longtime associates are a natural reaction to dealing with the unfamiliarity of changes they see happening. They are leery of new people placed in positions that influence the organization in ways they may not fully understand yet. They may feel they are losing control, turf, or even power, all of which can bring about uncomfortable and confusing emotions.

I've worked in organizations that implemented significant changes, and I witnessed firsthand how newcomers who were contributing to their advancement by being innovative and thinking outside the box may also make mistakes. They may push established boundaries because they're not familiar with them due to their short tenure. Or because they underestimate the norms that are part of the context of their corporate culture. Paradoxically, they were brought in precisely to do just that—to be agents of change.

Because these newcomers are rattling the status quo, the veterans may naturally view themselves as defenders of their well-established ways of working. They become protective and directly attack the actions of those they perceive to be dangerous to the organization's continued success. Another strategy may be for them to enlist those with power to join them in their mission to undermine the new hires who are seen as "rocking the boat."

For leaders managing a transition, this is a critical issue that requires attention and intervention. You need to be open and accessible to hearing and acknowledging your team's concerns. Your ability to actively listen will be crucial. In addition, you must stay on course, clarifying, communicating, and highlighting the importance of their collective role as leaders to be focused and help the company to navigate turbulent waters toward the desired future, with a collaborative sense of purpose.

Gui

By understanding the transformation—and wanting it to succeed—our long-time leaders were able to accept the idea of working with new associates who had a style vastly different from their own.

Of course, not everything went smoothly. There were times when our new hires took action without paying attention to certain controls and checks that we had put in place. This caused trouble and I had to intervene to fix these situations, to assure the company we were taking measures to have these leaders avoid repeating those errors in the future.

In such situations it might have been easier to simply ask someone who did not fit in to just leave, but my feeling was that this would not solve the issue. It was incumbent on us to train them and surround them with people who knew the rules and could guide them. At the same time, we had to create the possibility for them to bring to the transformation their entrepreneurial expertise, digital knowledge, and agile style—the very attributes we needed to successfully change. They also had to understand that risks that may be permitted in a start-up would not always be feasible in a company of our size and visibility.

As the CEO, I had to understand what that fine line was between what would and would not work for Walmex. The leader must be the one to take action, to assure everyone in the company that certain errors made by any team member will be corrected and not happen again. I believe in helping others learn from such situations just as I tried to learn from my own mistakes. This is the way our new associates began to personally change as they led change.

I spoke with Carlos about this in one of our coaching sessions, which occurred on a regular basis and were so valuable to me. Sometimes we met by Zoom, other times in person. For this session, Carlos and I met in the conference room, where we could have privacy. I mentioned to him the challenges of trying to integrate newcomers into the company. "They come to us from start-ups or digital companies, and sometimes have difficulty understanding the importance of controls we have in place, which they interpret as unnecessary bureaucracy."

Carlos responded, "I can imagine the difficulty of getting everyone on board and aligned to work for a common cause. I believe it may help to generate conditions that will lead to productive conversations with your whole team—the veterans as well as the digitally savvy newcomers."

When I asked him how to create such "conditions," he said, "Let me offer you a suggestion for the next time you have a similar opportunity. Gather the team together and open with a statement that explains exactly what you just told me—that a polarized perception exists about controls and procedures in the company. Then devote 30 to 45 minutes to the following exercise. Start by asking them to individually write down their answers to these two questions:

1. How can we maintain the "necessary" controls and procedures essential to the health of the business while deciding which ones we can dispense with if they go against the needs of the transformation?
2. What will help us continue learning from each other to further enhance our abilities as a team and individually as we step up to the challenges required to successfully lead the transformation?

"Next, ask them to form pairs or triads and share their answers. Continue with a whole group discussion and summarize their insights on flip charts."

Carlos added, "I believe the discussion itself will generate important insights, which will benefit everyone and help you reinforce their ability to collaborate on the common goals of the transformation. It will be necessary as you're honoring Sam Walton's vision for our modern times."

The whole process to integrate the new associates with the veterans wasn't easy, but I strongly believe it was worth the effort and risk. We began to have a great blend of people who were more open to each other's viewpoints and ideas and wanted to help their colleagues succeed. Instead of looking at how different we are, everyone started to see that together we formed a stronger team that could accomplish much more than we would individually. And both groups of professionals understood they were more capable as we made headway with the company's transformation.

Carlos

The leader who is the sponsor of change must gather the courage to protect the process of transformation as well as those who are forging new paths and, in doing so, spearheading the change. It is up to the leader to help those agents of change have a better understanding of the norms of the organization they are working to transform.

In Gui's case, his ability to show caring and conviction, and to lay himself on the line to defend the transformation and those who made errors in the process of implementing it, was an act of leadership courage. It enhanced his credibility instead of minimizing it.

Ironically, as everyone began to see the positive results of the initiatives of these change agents, the intensity of opposition against them started to diminish. As Gui once said to me, "It is easy to relish the successful outcomes, but no one wants to pay the price it took to get there."

The Human Connection

Carlos

As the title of our chapter indicates, there are many kinds of learning. Reverse mentoring was utilized as a development strategy to bridge the generational technology gap within the organization. Gui and I were engaged in executive coaching, a different developmental strategy to help him enhance his leadership potential and skills by targeting specific areas for improvement. What we worked on together in our coaching sessions was poles apart from the reverse mentoring Gui received to help him get up to speed on digital technology. Our focus was on how he could be more attuned to the needs of his team and gain a deeper behavioral self-awareness as well. It required committed, incremental work and consistent follow-up, but the results turned out to be life-changing.

Gui

The lessons I learned from Carlos taught me about the need to reach out to my team members. A leader has to understand the power of the job and how to achieve the right balance between listening to yourself and listening to others. I've witnessed CEOs who sometimes don't understand how easily self-confidence can turn into arrogance, and how insularity can become isolating.

Carlos

There are times that strengths can be misused, even abused, and a leader needs to recognize when to lean into a strength and when that kind of leaning in can become detrimental.

"Feedforward"

Gui

I've been in meetings that have been purely strategic and technical; I prefer to fertilize the human connection, reducing the psychological distance between myself and others. Some leaders listen only to the voice in their own head, thinking, *Nobody is going to tell me what to do.* These are the leaders who ultimately will fail because they don't have a clue how to inspire others, not recognizing that it is about becoming closer to the people you need to bring with you during any transition, not shutting them out or alienating them. Showing your vulnerability reveals your humanity and that can help change the dynamic of a suppressed, ineffective corporate meeting.

Carlos

Emotional self-disclosure can elevate a primarily intellectual or technical discussion to a more human common ground level that can facilitate communication and interaction. Most business meetings revolve around discussing performance indicators such as financial metrics, sales performance, market share, profitability, and liquidity. Sometimes, these discussions can become contentious and lead to disagreements among colleagues with different viewpoints. Such situations may result in a lack of participation or withdrawal, where people are not willing to express their thoughts or feelings or become passive-aggressive. In such scenarios, leaders can intervene by openly sharing what they perceive to be happening in the meeting and their feelings about it. This kind of self-disclosure can create a psychological safety net that encourages others to do the same, leading to more productive meeting interactions.

Gui

In my coaching sessions with Carlos, I began to understand that even though hearing feedback could be difficult, it was part of making that human connection, of putting aside ego, of becoming the leader I needed to be to lead change. Even if asking for feedback was risky and sometimes forced me to hear things I didn't necessarily want to hear, I knew it would ultimately give me more tools to use to be a more effective leader.

Carlos

The aim was to help Gui be a more effective leader. Maintaining consistent follow-up communication with his team members not only reinforced his efforts to achieve the behavioral changes he was seeking to make in himself but at the same time showed his consistent commitment to what he had promised to do, which helped to positively impact the perception his team members had of some of his leadership behaviors. However, this was not a slam dunk for Gui or, in my experience, for other executives I've worked with. One of the issues is how leaders conceptualize feedback. For example, Gui was equating it to a performance evaluation, which recently had not been a fun experience for him. He wondered about his capacity to deal with the information he received. Was he taking his willingness to be vulnerable to a perilous extreme? This kind of mindset may generate apprehension and avoidance.

My good friend Marshall Goldsmith, creator of the renowned Stakeholder Centered Coaching, offers a great antidote, which he calls "feedforward." He makes the point that "feedback" focuses on what occurred in the past, "not on the infinite variety of opportunities that can happen in the future."

Gui needed to benefit from shifting his mindset toward the fact that he cannot change the past. Instead, we worked on how he could focus on improving in the present and the future. In this way, he learned to seek positive and constructive suggestions from his team members so that he could continue making progress in the areas he had chosen to work on. By doing so, he began to strive for better performance going forward rather than dwelling on past behavioral slips. His stakeholders also found it easier and more constructive to help their leader be better and not focus solely on what he had done wrong.

Eduardo de la Garza, Chief Human Resources Officer, Walmex

Six months after the Exco meeting where we had discussed his behavior, Gui confidently walked into the conference room for our regular committee meeting. He surprised us by asking for a performance review.

He said, "I want to hear how I'm doing. Rate me from 1 to 5—no, from 1 to 10. Let me know if I'm getting better. Am I doing things differently? Am I making other kinds of errors?"

Gui is a CEO who can put aside his ego in order to perform well. He had an awareness that he needed to change and a willingness to do it and to do follow-up to make sure he continued to make progress. One of the things I remember him saying was, "Challenge me more. What else can I do better?"

We came up with a plan that we would signal to him if we thought his tone was becoming rude. After some brainstorming we landed on the idea of sending him simple messages using colors—red for "stop," yellow for "caution," and green for "you're good." I personally started communicating with him on WhatsApp, sending him a red signal when I thought it was necessary, or when someone had texted me that he was getting out of line.

For example, one time, Gui was speaking to someone who challenged him on one of the points he had proposed. The executive began by saying, "I don't agree with your decision about how to move forward."

This man went through his reasons, and as soon as he finished, Gui spoke up, his voice rising. "This isn't personal, but your reasons for disagreeing with me are bullshit. When you are CEO and have my experience, you can have the last word. But for now, I do."

I quickly sent Gui a text with a red signal. I could tell he saw it and soon after he apologized to the executive.

He and I have a circle of trust that allows me to push back with him. We agree that we should always engage in logical and rational feedback, using facts to express ourselves. Then we make recommendations and it always seems to work out.

Gui

I was still learning how to listen and respond more appropriately but I noticed that others were changing too—they were learning to read me better, to become more attuned to my behavior in ways that also made our mutual communication better.

Carlos

People assimilate how to make change work for themselves in a variety of ways. Gui's team became more adept at not pushing his buttons. They recognized approaches they could take that would lead to more effective outcomes rather than just more stress. These reciprocal changes helped Gui and his team become cohesive and they collaborated more effectively as the organizational transformation accelerated.

The Value of Working with a Coach

Gui

One of the lessons I learned from working with Carlos is that the path toward transformative self-awareness can be made more effective with the support of an experienced guide. The CEO who thinks they can see themselves with laser-sharp clarity may in fact be unaware of the blind spots that will prevent them from truly being successful—in changing themselves or their company. While Carlos and I recognize that circumstances may not always allow leaders to work with an executive coach, it is nevertheless important to keep in mind the value of having one if that becomes a possibility. Realizing that we can't do everything on our own keeps us humble and provides us with a reason to reach out to those we trust—whether it's a professional coach, a colleague, or a mentor. They can help us interpret the feedback from people on our team and see things we might miss.

When Carlos was first brought into Walmex in 2017 it was to help coach members of my team, but over time he began to specialize his efforts to help CEOs worldwide. So we decided he would focus solely on coaching me, especially after I received the negative appraisal from my boss. We hired Pedro Langre as the new coach for my team in September 2018 and that's what allowed Carlos to concentrate more in-depth on coaching me during these many months of the transition.

Carlos helped me understand that when it came to feedback, my direct reports were not trying to undermine me with their comments—they were trying to help me understand that I needed to get out of my own way. I initially misread their critiques as criticism when in fact it was an affirmation that they believed I had the potential to do things better. They had faith that I had it in me to improve my own leadership behavior as I tackled the monumental task of transforming Walmex. But it took Carlos's patient coaching and wise insights to help me shift my perspective so that I could approach feedback with discernment instead of becoming defensive.

With his guidance, I learned how to become more approachable so that my team felt they could speak directly to me about how I could improve. I wouldn't have fully realized the steps I needed to take to act on their feedback without his guidance. He provided me with a fresh perspective so I could see the impact of my words and actions and understand that even small changes could yield major results.

Carlos

The importance of executive leaders having a clear understanding of an organization's purpose, vision, mission, values, and strategic goals cannot be overstated. In our experience, this provides a solid foundation for aligning the leadership behavior changes aimed for in the coaching process.

In the following section, we include suggestions on how to make the coaching experience productive, and we offer a checklist of questions to ask a potential coach, in the same way that investment guides provide readers with essential questions to ask financial advisors. While it's not necessary to have a coach to make use of the many leadership lessons of this book, we feel it's important for readers to see it as a valuable option in their repertoire of tools. As you will see from the excerpts of our coaching sessions presented throughout *Reinventing the Leader*, the experience of recognizing the need and asking for help is a necessary first step in learning to listen. By developing empathic concern for those who depend on your leadership, you'll be better equipped to help them accomplish their aims.

Making the Most of Your Coaching Experience:
- Develop a clear and compelling picture of the leadership improvement you want to achieve. Is it aligned with the company's purpose? What will success look like?
- Know that commitment and dedication to a productive learning process will be required.
- Plan for a rigorous 360-degree assessment of your leadership behaviors, which may include comprehensive interviews with your key stakeholders—boss, colleagues, direct reports, customers, and others as appropriate. This will identify leadership strengths as well as possible behaviors to change.
- With the information obtained from the assessments, choose one or two behaviors that if improved will provide significant value and benefit. Underpromise but overdeliver!
- Develop a detailed action plan that identifies specific goals for the behaviors selected, with clear action steps, potential obstacles to remove, people who can provide support and assistance, and success indicators for each goal.
- Share your plan with your stakeholders and assure them of your commitment to change.
- Work with your coach to identify and remove conscious and unconscious resistance to change and attach your heart to your efforts to accomplish your goals.
- Commit to frequently seeking feedback and suggestions from stakeholders on selected behaviors to improve. Allow them to support and help you in your efforts to change.
- Be open and transparent with your coach. Share your feedback about what is working and what is not working with your coaching process.

Questions to Ask a Potential Coach:
1. Can you tell me about your professional training and how you became a coach?
2. What areas of development are your specialties?
3. What is your coaching philosophy?

4. I want to improve in [specific areas of development]. What is your experience and approach to coaching leaders in these areas?
5. What assessment tools do you use? Will you interview stakeholders?
6. What will be the frequency of our coaching sessions, and how long will the engagement be for?
7. Will our sessions be in person, by phone, or by videoconference?
8. How will progress toward my goals be measured?

Additionally, Determine:

- Credibility of the person as a coach, years of experience coaching executives, success track record, organizations, and references
- The coach's ability to quickly establish rapport with you
- The coach's interpersonal skills
- The confidentiality of the information you'll share
- How to avoid overdependence on the coach

Gui

It's important to also emphasize that self-change is a never-ending process. Even now, I still wrestle with trying to be better. Just when I think I've taken two steps forward, I may take one step back. The key is to be vigilant and to recognize when you're not living up to your personal goals despite your best efforts. As we've said earlier, it's about progress, not perfection.

For us in 2017 and 2018, the transformation was about changing ourselves as we changed the company. Our mission was to make it more convenient for people's needs to be met when they shopped, whether in our stores or online. At that time, we could not have imagined that redefining the company's entire operations would eventually lead us to think more broadly about making a difference in every aspect of our customers' lives. It wouldn't just be about selling them a TV but offering them opportunities to get Wi-Fi and health services and even a gym membership, all at affordable prices. Ultimately, we would expand on Sam Walton's original customer-centric intention by using new methodologies and leveraging technological advances to accomplish that goal. Over the course of the next five years, we would push the boundaries of the possible, never losing sight of our primary focus, which was to always put our customers and our people first.

LEARNING POINTS FOR SUCCESSFUL LEADERS

Reinventing Yourself to Transform Your Company

Reinventing Yourself

- **Lesson:** Understand the power of your job and that you must balance listening to yourself with listening to others. It doesn't matter how much you know and how experienced you are; you will always benefit from other perspectives.

> "Listen with the will to learn."
> —Unarine Ramaru

- **Lesson:** The more your team knows you and you know your team, the more you will listen to and understand each other. Having the courage to disclose your feelings creates an environment where people want to help each other.

> "It is teamwork that remains the ultimate competitive advantage, both because it is so powerful and so rare."
> —Patrick Lencioni

- **Lesson:** The journey toward transformative self-awareness can be made more effective by working with an experienced coach. A professional coach can help you understand your strengths and opportunities better and faster as well as to help you change and improve. Using your strengths can be a very powerful tool to help you correct what needs to be fixed.

> "Coaching is unlocking a person's potential to maximize their growth."
> —Sir John Whitmore

- **Lesson:** Be open to learning from anyone and be thankful to them. The important thing is not who's more senior but who can teach you about something you don't know.

> "You're never going to learn something as
> profoundly as when it's purely out of curiosity."
> —Christopher Nolan

Transform Your Company

- **Lesson:** Any change brings risk, but the biggest risk is not to change. Some people are willing to take risks before others, and senior leaders need to recognize them and give them space to grow.

> "It is better to be boldly decisive and risk being wrong
> than to agonize at length and be right too late."
> —Marilyn Moats Kennedy

- **Lesson:** Antibodies defend us from strange invaders. The same happens inside companies, and the CEO and other senior leaders must help those "invaders" become part of the team.

> "It is not the manager's job to prevent risks. It is the
> manager's job to make it safe to take them."
> —Ed Catmull

- **Lesson:** We all score goals and make mistakes. The beauty of the error is the learning that can come from it, allowing us to make things right and become stronger than before.

> "I skated, fell down, and learned to pick
> myself up in front of millions."
> —Michelle Kwan

The Three Questions

Gui

The magnitude of the change at Walmex was enormous. When it came time to put into place the people who would lead the next chapter of the organization, we found it was a challenging thing to do. The partner at the global consulting company we were working with suggested a fairly quick way to gain the information we needed in order to assess who would be best for all the leadership roles we had to fill. I was surprised by the simplicity of what he proposed and the effectiveness of it once we put it to the test.

The consultant told us that by asking the following three questions we could assess the readiness and willingness of people who worked for the company to see which ones would best contribute to the transformation.

- *Do you understand the change?*
- *Do you want to make the change?*
- *Are you able to make the change?*

The answer to each question gave me an understanding of the person's mindset—did they feel they knew what the company would be undertaking? Did they personally feel excited to be part of this journey? And last, but certainly not least, did they feel up to the challenge? The questions did not simply apply to the organization's transformation, but the person's own willingness to go through what would inevitably be a personal transformation as well.

As I discovered in the months to come, these questions—and each individual's answers to them—would provide valuable information about their comfort level in being part of the changes ahead.

In this chapter we'll explore how the three questions combine with six essential business principles to form a vital equation—the questions allowing an employee or associate to express their desire to go the extra mile on the journey and the six principles translating that passion into action. As you'll see, the six principles equip us with the tools we need to develop a synchronized plan and deliver it. From expression to execution, the questions and principles are the formula every leader and associate can use to achieve success, whether for a strategic initiative or a major transformation.

Former Partner, Global Consulting Company

I was a consultant specializing in Enterprise Agility at a global consulting firm. My role was to be the leader to coach Walmex on their transformation, which had never been attempted anywhere by a retailer of their scale, with 6,000 employees at the company.

It was important for people to believe in the mission. Let me use a religious analogy here. If you can't understand the values associated with a certain faith, you can't really be a believer. The same thing applies to any form of transformation.

An organization is a collection of people, and they have their own rhythms and rituals they employ to get work done. Gui appreciated that to change his team's established mindset he needed to align them with an aspiration, starting small and then scaling it up. There needs to be a willingness among people to make this fundamental change, and not everyone is willing or cut out to go through it.

Change management lies at the heart of a transformation and Gui excelled at that, at setting up the right expectations among his team up front, letting them know what was expected and that not everyone would make the cut.

Some people said yes to all three questions, but it became obvious they didn't have the skills to adapt and think strategically. The transformation involved such massive changes that it forced people to say whether it was working for them or not. Some realized there wasn't a path forward for them and said, "I'll move on."

Carlos

In determining which team members would be part of the transformation, there were a number of important variables to consider. In addition to the three questions, other considerations included: What knowledge would they be required to already have? Would they need external help? Did they have experience with the issues involved in the process? What motivational factors should be considered? Did they have the confidence to carry out the tasks? What level of commitment would they be willing to make to perform their responsibilities? What were the incentives someone needed to achieve their tasks? Answers to these questions would complement the three questions and give Gui more information about the task-readiness of members of his team.

I had the good fortune and privilege to know and learn from Dr. Paul Hersey, who collaborated with Dr. Ken Blanchard to develop a theory that became known as Situational Leadership®. Years later, Blanchard et al. created a revised model, calling it SLII®. A fundamental component of Situational Leadership is the concept of *readiness*, which he defined as "the degree of demonstrated ability and willingness to *accept, own*, and *perform*" (emphasis added) specific tasks. (Notice the relationship to the three questions: *Do you understand the change? Do you want to make the change? Are you able to make the change?*)

Determining these factors is what Situational Leadership refers to as "assessing readiness," and the three questions the consultant provided to Gui would turn out to be invaluable in helping him gauge the readiness of individual team members. In addition, Gui would be able to adapt his own leadership behavior to lead them more effectively.

Gui

We were asking a lot from people and we had to know if they would be valuable contributors to this collaborative effort or if, for whatever reason, they did not feel they could join us in such a massive transformation. Some paid lip service to wanting to help us reach our goals, but I emphasized that it was important for them to express how they really felt so we could know their true level of commitment.

Carlos

Gui and I discussed the challenges involved in attempting to initiate a large-scale change in an organization that is doing well and doesn't perceive a reason to change or transform itself. It's critical for leaders to answer such questions from their team as: What is the compelling reason for the change? Why is it important and why now? How will it affect our staff? They will need as much clarity as possible about the *significance* of embarking on such a potentially disruptive process.

I told Gui that a lot of preparation was being done to help people be at peak readiness for the implementation phase. However, they would continue to need guidance and direction, and they needed to know they could count on Gui. Most importantly, they could work with their peers who may be further ahead on the learning curve regarding some of the tasks they would be required to deliver on.

Former Partner, Global Consulting Company

You can coach someone who lacks certain skills to learn to be good at something—for example, sales—role-modeling behavior for them. But the question is: Are they willing to do the work? Do they *want* to do it?

One's adaptive mindset is the key metric you need to measure to see if someone will be a high performer in the transformation.

I remember seeing a video of Steve Jobs, an interview that he did in 1996, months before he went back to Apple. They asked him at that time what he would do to help the company, which was in trouble.

Would he cut costs? No, he replied. "The way out is not to slash and burn," but to rely on innovation for future growth. You need people who will help the organization do that.

In any company there are 5% of people who believe in growth and innovation as a way of leaving a legacy. The other 95% are primarily interested in pleasing their bosses, of maintaining the status quo and toeing the line to achieve career growth. These are two very different paths, two different mindsets. And the fact is you need a balance of both. Too many innovators and they trip over each other's toes. Too many of the 95 percenters and the company dies a slow death.

The question is: What does someone want as their personal legacy? You need to get those 5% in a position to change things.

Carlos

I had told Gui that if his team was going to make the changes that would be required of them, they would need as much information as possible about their significance and importance. At Walmex, people were accustomed to having clear guidelines established by senior leadership, pointing them in the direction they needed to go (just think of Moses in the Bible leading the Israelites to the Promised Land), but Gui invited his team to join him in answering the questions together. He was more comfortable than his collaborators were in sitting with ambiguity and uncertainty. But this was an organization that had been used to precision and order. Gui's more flexible, informal, adapt-as-you-go style was not very reassuring to them. The associates were outstanding at implementing things, but they expected to get specific instructions rather than be part of the more elusive creative process.

Gui

The capacity to thrive in a state of ambiguity is very important when there are disruptive changes in the world of business. Uncertainty can paralyze some, but it can energize others. My new boss at the company was Judith McKenna, president and CEO of Walmart International, and she once told me that where others see problems, I see opportunities. I believe that is the main reason I can cope so well with uncertainty. I believe we can always benefit from change and do better than we did the day before. When you are too afraid of getting things wrong, you fail to seize the possibilities that present themselves. I worked hard to help my team develop more tolerance for the possibility of failure when trying new things, and at the same time I also had to try to create more clarity about the risks we needed to take and why.

Guideposts for the Journey

*"The most important days of your life are the day you
are born and the day you find out why."*
—Mark Twain

Gui

Once we had gauged the readiness of our team to meet the complex demands of the transformation, we needed to make sure they had the tools they needed to succeed. Readiness without a road map can lead to someone getting lost—taking wrong turns and making unnecessary mistakes. The three questions help to determine will and capability, but how do you create guideposts for an effective path forward?

Some companies define their future based on their past. They project the past onto the future, happy with their current performance and certain that if they continue to do the same things, they will generate the same results. Other companies believe their best strategy is to make small adjustments to areas not performing well, allowing them to perform better in the future. In both cases, the company's future is dependent on what was done before and this is a recipe for failure, in the medium and long term.

I prefer companies that look 10 to 20 years ahead to define what they want to be, and then they come back to the present to define how to reach that desired destination. Their past helped them get where they are and may have developed some much-needed capabilities *but* it's not the most important contributor to the future. *A company must create its future not by looking backward but forward.*

The world is changing fast—customers change fast and so do their needs and pain points. At the same time, competitors change and new ones arise.

As we ramped up our efforts to transform Walmex, Carlos and I drew on our combined decades of experience to identify six principles that we saw as essential to staying on the right path in business, whether during the kind of dramatic transformation we were experiencing or the day-to-day running of a company that is not undergoing any significant disruptions but still needs the best tools to succeed: purpose, passion, strategy, talent, synchronization, and delivery. These would be the touchstones that would guide us on the turbulent journey ahead.

The three questions that became so fundamental to building the right team for the transformation were reinforced by these six principles. The questions measured understanding, willingness, and capability and the six principles translated those essential qualities into action.

The principles were effectively the result of everything I had learned over the course of my career, and I use them as the practical tools to manage and lead as a CEO. If you know someone understands the mission, wants to be part of it, and is capable of doing what it takes to make it happen, the natural next step is creating an action plan: a basis for turning willingness and readiness into real-world priorities. In our case, we had to make sure that there was a clear alignment between each individual's personal values and the purpose of the company as it implements every phase of the transformation.

Our team needed to translate purpose into strategy. To understand and like the strategy in order to be able to deliver it, which is where talent and synchronization come into play. This is often the most challenging part of the equation because so many things can go sideways. Where talent is concerned, those with the most innovative ideas may be the ones who are criticized the most. It is the leader's job to protect them, to give them the space they need to be creative, while at the same time making sure everyone feels they're being heard. Even in the face of conflicts that may occur, leaders need to make sure everyone resolves their differences and works collaboratively for the good of the mission. For that's ultimately the goal for leaders and their team—to successfully make the changes necessary to better serve their customers.

The way I conduct business is based on these six principles. I do not believe in a magic formula for winning that's valid for every company, every moment, and every team; nevertheless, I do believe that these ingredients can increase the chance of succeeding.

Purpose

Gui

Midway through the transformation process, I did an exercise to define what my purpose is, using methodology developed by team leadership coach Pedro Langre. Working with Carlos and Pedro, I discovered that my purpose is to live, love, and have an impact.

I admit I live with enormous energy, absorbing everything that life gives to me. I always say, "I love what I do, and I do it with tremendous intensity." I try to transmit this passion and sense of purpose to others, mobilizing them to do what I believe needs to be done.

I express love with intensity too. I love caring for people and looking after them; I also like to be loved and cared for. I'm always surprised when people write to me saying that they admire the fact that I am very human and care for others. It's surprising for me to read this because I assume everyone feels the same way about helping people.

One of the issues I needed to manage better about my own behavior involved my reaction when I perceived that someone was not acting in good faith or with the right intention. I had an emotional, visceral response to that. I still do sometimes. Which just shows that the work we need to do to reinvent ourselves never ends.

Another aspect that is part of my overall sense of purpose is the desire to have an impact, to make things happen, to influence an outcome. I'm driven to succeed, to learn and innovate, and to create value. I read and study every chance I get, and I work hard to improve myself, the business, and the people that work with me. I teach them, yes, but I learn from them too.

Just like humans, companies also need to have a purpose, a reason to exist, and this is different from making profits. The purpose should influence a company's values and strategy and be top of mind in every decision that management makes. Companies that have a clearly defined sense of purpose achieve more, and their employees tend to be more inspired to meet the established goals. Some companies, with the help of consultants, come up with an artificial purpose that doesn't represent what its people believe, and this never works over the long term. There must be harmony between the purpose and the intrinsic values of the company. You'll want to feel that where you work reflects your values and purpose too. Otherwise, should you really be there?

Passion

Gui

I either love what I do or I don't. This passion energizes me and helps me to be resilient in the face of challenges. I believe passion is a necessary component of accomplishing more and succeeding. When we align our passion with a powerful purpose it can give us the inner strength and direction to attempt extraordinary things.

I know people I work with refer to me as "passionate" and it's true. But it's linked to the purpose at hand; if I believe in it, I get passionate about it. The same will be true of the people you work with.

Strategy

Gui

I believe that we should create our future by defining what we want to be in the long term, whether it be 10 or 20 years from now. That vision should be independent of what we are today, but it has to be linked to our purpose. Once we have crystallized what we want the company to look like, we have to work backward and identify the capabilities, talent, experiences, products, and services that we need to have in place in order to achieve that desired future.

To reach that goal you need to think about the main things you have to do and also clearly define what you are *not* going to do. This is always the most difficult part as we are often tempted to do more than we are able. Your criteria should be to take on only what helps you build your future. Never try to do more than your operational capacity as this is the shortest route to failure.

In thinking long term, you have to give yourself enough time to think big, free of the limits that may currently constrain the company. As you get clarity, you'll need to go back to the short term (let's say, the next 12 months) to build a detailed plan so people know exactly what they need to do in the next few months. That's why I hate three-to-five-year plans—they are neither long enough to reimagine the future nor short-term enough to know what you have to do tomorrow.

As I considered long-term goals for the company, I realized that the same principle applies to us. We have to imagine where we want to be far enough in the future to begin building plans to get there now. A lot of people who come to talk to me about their careers spend most of the available time telling me what they did in the past and then they want my opinion about what I think their next step should be. I always ask them to talk to me about their long-term, desired future; if they don't have a vision of that in mind, how can they know if the next steps they take will be the right ones?

Let me tell you a story from my own professional life. Years before becoming CEO, I was offered a great job opportunity that I had to refuse because it would not have helped me to achieve my goals. Yes, it was a promotion, with more money, but it likely would have moved me away from the vision I had of where I wanted to be and from my purpose as well. I tell people, "If you don't know where you want to go, any bus can take you there."

The scarcest resource we have is time, and so wasting your or the company's time by doing things that don't contribute to the future is the worst possible action. Often, once you decide what you want and define the things you have to do to get there, you realize you don't have the time needed to do everything. The only thing you must not do is waste time. I never arrived for a new job 100% ready, but I was always sufficiently prepared. The rest I learned on the job.

No matter what business you're running and team you're leading, if you're searching for your strategy, define your future and the way to get there and stay focused on that. You can adjust as necessary, but always "keep your eyes on the prize."

Talent

Gui

As a leader you need to have the right talent for the future you want to build. Sometimes you have it; other times you have to develop the needed capabilities among the team you have; and in certain situations you need to buy, rent, or create a joint venture to acquire it. After defining your long-term vison, figure out the talent you need and work hard to get them on board. This is where many companies fall short, especially if they have been very successful in previous years.

People are capable of change, but this sometimes takes time and effort. At Walmex, our reverse mentoring program was working well, though we knew results would be incremental and that we had to be patient to let everyone learn at their own pace. The most difficult situation is when a leader needs to say goodbye to people who have contributed to the company's success in the past but are not able to help it achieve its future goals. It's human nature for us to take longer than we should to accept that such people will be impediments to the growth that's required. The sooner we recognize it, the better it is for those people and for the company. Though they may no longer fit the company's needs, they often find another company where their capabilities are an excellent match and it's a win-win all around.

I'm an advocate for diversifying the talent pool. Hiring people with only one kind of background or perspective makes the workplace more insular. But choosing a wide range of people helps to enrich debate and creates the opportunity to have different points of view, which leads to better decisions. Whether you're building a team for a complex transition as we were or simply staffing up a business, it is important that the CEO and other senior executives actively participate in the company's recruitment process to ensure it gets the right mix of people.

Synchronization

Gui

Once you have established purpose, passion, strategy, and talent for the company's transformation, then synchronization comes into play to explain it to the talent. Since I would often use the word *synchronization*, one of my previous bosses once asked me what I meant by it. I said, "It's like we're all in the same boat. We need to row in the same direction at the same speed. If we row in opposite directions, the boat goes nowhere, and if we go at different speeds, that's a waste of energy and time. Now that we have our strategy, our job is to make sure everyone understands it, is willing to be part of it, and not only knows how to help deliver it but is capable of doing it well." That's synchronization, and the strategy needs to be end-to-end instead of continuing with silos, which would not have worked effectively as we moved toward greater collaboration.

Grouping people into silos in a company has always been a problem. They can solve problems or improve things but only based on their own areas of interest, without looking at the implications such change or actions will have on the rest of the business. The agile way of working requires an interdependent, end-to-end view where all interactions are seen and considered. Throughout our own journey toward transformation, this issue was part of the diagnostic, the solution, and a key part of the implementation. Our efforts would not have succeeded if we had not moved to an agile methodology. You may find that this is the optimal approach for your business as well, creating a more collaborative business environment no matter what the situation is.

Former Partner, Global Consulting Company

Gui's personal evolution as he made this journey of transformation was a learning experience for me too. He understood that this was about more than becoming a digital organization; it was about becoming an agile organization. I knew he had already spent a year and a half steeping himself in the subject, visiting digital labs and companies that used technology—absorbing ING's digital transformation and the trends coming out of Silicon Valley—and gaining a good grasp of the art of the possible. But he realized early on that he had to balance *a transition in mindset* with a change in operations. I don't know many leaders who would have appreciated that, but Gui did. And he helped me to do so too.

Gui

A surprising, and frankly remarkable, event occurred as we were shifting to an agile methodology. We were having difficulty recruiting and retaining agile coaches to work with the numbers of people we needed to train. While we were waiting for a new tech leader to join us, the people who had been part of his small group temporarily started reporting to me. At one of our meetings, they shared that they had developed a game to teach others how to use agile methodology and they had been playing it in our company canteen. They told me that they had already successfully trained 500 associates! When I heard they had *voluntarily* organized this and that people were so enthusiastic about learning this new methodology, I knew the transformation had begun to catch on within the entire company.

Delivery

Gui

The sixth element after purpose, passion, strategy, talent, and synchronization is delivery. It's the action we take to fulfill our ambitions. This is in some ways the most difficult step. The previous five ingredients are essential but they're still not enough to achieve the end goal: delivery of an end-to-end solution in a unified way.

Part of the challenge is that delivery involves different people in different areas fully aligning: they must have a clear sense of why we need to deliver, what needs to be done, and how they're expected to contribute to the process. What I said to my previous boss about synchronization applies here but with an added element: not only do all the rowers in the boat need to row in the same direction and at the same pace, but they also must *understand* the destination they need to reach. That new shore matters to everybody involved. If it were just for financial gain, that might not be enough but, as we discussed earlier, when it's personally meaningful—a matter of a higher goal—then it becomes a mission that's unstoppable.

Inspiring a team to see *why* the transformation is so consequential is more art than science. This is where the CEO must lead the way, finding opportunities to articulate the strategy with an aspirational message that is exceptionally clear and choosing the right talent to get the job done. Hopefully, the leader also has the charisma to convince people that this is the way to go, achieving the buy-in that is crucial to make sure the whole team is rowing at the same speed in the same direction.

For successful delivery, we needed to communicate the strategy effectively, design detailed plans to accomplish it, and constantly monitor progress, changing what needed to be changed as the need arose. This is an exercise that never ends as we always have to evolve the strategy and the plans. However, the one constant is the purpose—that remains the North Star that guides us. You will find that alignment, which is a crucial part of delivery and is a result of making a higher goal your driving force, will make a difference in the leadership of your team as well.

The "Gui Factor"

Carlos

When it came time for Gui to help people see why the transformation went beyond the bottom line, he relied on what was known within the company as the "Gui Factor," his genuine, contagiously passionate energy. He has a remarkable capacity to connect with people on a human level. At that moment in time, we needed everyone to "get" the transformation, not just intellectually but emotionally.

Gui

When people speak of the "Gui Factor," I think they're really talking about the energy, charisma, and enthusiasm they perceive I have, which is fueled by my passion and purpose. It's what helps me convince people to join me on the journey, to move in the direction I'm advocating.

Throughout my career, many people have expressed admiration for the fact that, despite being in a senior position, I remain approachable and empathetic toward others. I believe they are referring to my tendency to prioritize the well-being and success of those around me. I have devoted a significant amount of time to sharing my knowledge and experience, mentoring others, and taking a long-term perspective on the business. My willingness to work hard and deliver positive results, as well as my transparency in my dealings with others, are key factors in building strong relationships. As I have previously mentioned, trust is built on honesty, reliability, and care, and I feel that by earning that trust I've inspired others to speak about "the Gui Factor."

Eduardo de la Garza, Chief Human Resources Officer, Walmex

One of Gui's most impressive qualities as a leader is that he knows just what to say to connect with others, whether it's individually or a crowd of 1,000. Also, he can tell a story that puts everything into focus. There's one that I remember that was quite beautiful. Gui shared it when we had a forecasting meeting to decide on the budget for our separate departments. A number of us were stating what we would need for the future, and the discussion got very heated. Everybody was fighting, competing for the money we each needed to have for our departments. Instead of getting upset, Gui quietly told us this story:

When he was 10 years old and going to elementary school, he and his older brothers were talking with their father about what they would need for the new school year. One said, "I need 10 pesos for all my supplies," another said the same thing, and so did young Gui. They all needed money for lunch and transportation and books. Their father looked at them and said, "Congratulations, you each will get five pesos. That is all I can afford."

Without raising his voice or taking a rude tone, Gui calmed the room down. That story helped us to act maturely as we continued with our budget forecast. We each had to make compromises, knowing there was only so much we could each get.

It was a learning experience. Gui taught us to think more broadly, beyond the needs of our own individual departments. And there was a transformation on both sides.

That story was so effective that I have used it myself in meetings I've led.

Carlos

These qualities in Gui's personality inspired and attracted people from inside and outside the company to form a growing cadre of enthusiastic followers. People gladly came to join the transformation project that Gui envisioned because he offered them a seat at the table, a chance to work on a project aligned with their dreams and aspirations. They liked the way he made them feel valued and uniquely capable of contributing to the creation of something transcendental, in this case transforming one of the largest business organizations in Mexico and Central America. One of these key collaborators explained what had convinced her to work with Gui: "He was someone who cared about people and their ideas. I saw him as a leader with great potential for making a significant difference and leaving a positive legacy."

Former Partner, Global Consulting Company

Gui is that rare breed of leader who sees their own career growth as being about "shaking the status quo and growing the business," which is done via innovation.

When I started working with Gui, I saw he had a clear desire to push this transformation through, even though it was August and Walmex was getting close to peak selling season, with the holidays coming up. People at the company were very busy and there was a lot of discussion among his team about trying to find time for the workshops and meetings that would be necessary. Gui was determined to move forward. He told the team, "If it's hard to find time, we can schedule workshops on weekends," which elicited a jaw-dropping response. From me too. People immediately cleared their calendars to make time during the workweek. *We will make this happen* was Gui's message to everyone.

I've led five of these transformations, but none of them involved a retailer the size of Walmex. This kind of major change, transitioning to an end-to-end system, and applying a cross-functional process across multiple departments, was uncharted territory.

Gui brought simplicity to the process and he has the ability to understand concepts and clearly communicate them to his team. I could tell he was very conscious of time and wanted to set a target date to get the transformation done. He appreciated, even before I did, that he had only a finite amount of time to accomplish this transformation. That he needed to move fast. And, of course, later events like the pandemic—things beyond anyone's control—proved that he was right in his judgment.

He was a busy man running a huge business. I remember that in early 2019 I was having a conversation with him and asked him about his holidays. "Oh, I was working on Christmas," he said. That was the kind of commitment he had. No matter how much he was dealing with, Gui was willing to dedicate the time that was needed for this transformation. As a coach, I see other leaders who don't commit that kind of time to getting involved. They're just not willing to, but Gui was.

Former Partner, Global Consulting Company

When you look at leaders, the question is: Do they have the intrinsic strength to be able to make a change? Do they have the willingness and intent to dedicate time to it? To help their team have a more adaptive mindset? Gui has that intrinsic strength. He's respected across all sectors and he was willing to spend his social/political capital to make the transformation happen. He understood there were no guarantees that this would work. As I mentioned before, no retailer the size of Walmex had ever attempted and achieved a transformation at such scale.

But another important intrinsic strength Gui has is empathy, an ability to connect with people. I was once at a meeting where people needed to pair up to do an activity. Gui teamed up with someone he had recently had to let go. You'd think the guy would be pissed off, but he and Gui were laughing and at the end of the activity they hugged. That's because of Gui's genuine warmth.

Now that I'm running my own company, I find inspiration in leaders who've made smart decisions. I'd say 30 to 40% of my examples come from Gui.

Carlos

Even Gui, who had the bold courage to embark on the equivalent of an unknown wilderness journey toward a not-very-well-defined "promised land," experienced moments of anxiety. There was so much on the line. Such high stakes. I remember one meeting in particular during which Gui shared these feelings.

Gui

The main concern I had was about the size of the change combined with the size of Walmex. We had learned from other traditional companies that had gone through similar transformations, visiting their offices to understand firsthand how they had accomplished such a change, but they were all much smaller than our organization. When I met with Carlos, he asked how I was doing now that the company was about to ramp up its implementation efforts.

I said, "I've been preparing myself, the executive team, and the rest of the company for this transformation for a long time. But I must confess that as we approach the implementation phase, I'm becoming a little bit nervous. This is my career at stake . . ."

Carlos replied, "Gui, you and the team did a great job of preparing the company for it. You've taken all the necessary steps to make it happen as smoothly as possible, but we both know it's not going to be smooth. This is an important and necessary change that has been well planned and tested, and now it's time to move forward. Risks are always present, but the team has reduced the possibility that the business will experience a bad outcome."

"I agree," I said. As always, he was being honest and also reassuring. Still, since we were now closer to putting all our plans into action, I wondered if we would get the results we not only hoped for but needed to achieve. I confided in him, saying, "I can't escape from the anxiety and fear. I know we'll need to adjust things on the go, and I do believe this is the right move, but . . ." I wasn't even able to finish the sentence.

Carlos understood and said, "You'll do a great job. Stay focused on the company's mission, its purpose, its reason for being that was first established by Sam Walton."

He was reminding me of what mattered. Purpose. Passion. Having an impact. Now we would see if all the study, preparation, and risk would pay off and if this unprecedented effort could really succeed.

LEARNING POINTS FOR SUCCESSFUL LEADERS

Reinventing Yourself to Transform Your Company

Reinventing Yourself

- **Lesson:** When you align your passion with your purpose, it can give you the inner strength and direction to achieve extraordinary things.

  > "Your dreams are the blueprints of your soul.
  > They should take you by the hand and lead you
  > toward your life's purpose and passion."
  > —Mac Anderson

- **Lesson:** A key ingredient of self-reinvention is identifying those you can learn from and humbly drink from their fountains of knowledge and experience.

  > "Knowledge is not power. It's only potential power. It
  > only becomes power when we apply it and use it."
  > —Jim Kwik

- **Lesson:** You grow as a leader when you dig deep and commit to being the best version of yourself, particularly when heading up organizational change.

  > "If you don't build your dream, someone else
  > will hire you to help them build theirs."
  > —Dhirubhai Ambani

Transform Your Company

- **Lesson:** In a transformation, you need to give your team an aspirational, meaningful purpose to change their previously established way of thinking and working.

"Inspiration is not garnered from the litanies of what may
befall us; it resides in humanity's willingness to restore,
redress, reform, rebuild, recover, reimagine, and reconsider."
—Paul Hawken

- **Lesson:** In a major change, you should be looking for an adaptive mindset as a key measure of whether someone will be a high performer.

"Adaptability enforces creativity, and
creativity is adaptability."
—Pearl Zhu

- **Lesson:** When considering who will contribute most effectively to the change process, utilize the three questions in this chapter to make sure people understand the transformation, want to be part of it, and are able to act on it.

"Change is inevitable, but transformation
is by conscious choice."
—HeatherAsh Amara

- **Lesson:** For a successful transformation, you need to balance changing your team's mindset with changing their operations.

"What I dream of is an art of balance."
—Henri Matisse

- **Lesson:** Nowadays it's important for a leader to convey clarity even more than certainty—your team must have a clear sense of *why* they need to deliver, *what* needs to be done, and *how* they're expected to deliver.

"Clarity is the most important thing . . . if you
are not clear, nothing is going to happen."
—Diane von Furstenberg

7

Orchestrating the Pace

"Adopt the pace of nature: her secret is patience."
—Ralph Waldo Emerson

Gui

The fears I had expressed to Carlos were based on all the unknowns ahead of us. It's natural to feel this way as you approach a time of major change. Fear can even help—causing you to carefully consider all options—as long as it doesn't make you freeze.

As Nelson Mandela said, "I learned that courage was not the absence of fear, but the triumph over it." I was fortunate to have Carlos as my coach; he helped me develop a wider view of the situation, to look at my feelings in context of the process of leading change. He helped me to see that to immerse myself in learning was a way to triumph over my fears, and to act by using what I learned to take calculated risks.

Transformation is risky when it's not done wisely. I have watched companies lose market share when they didn't keep their own core principles in focus. A brand can suffer when the very concept that made it successful is sidelined and other messaging takes over that shifts people's perception of it. Walmart's values are part of why it is an iconic company, and in my role as CEO I knew that for all the changes we'd be making we literally could not afford to disrupt what we stood for—making people's lives better. I had to make sure that for every step forward we weren't taking two steps back in terms of delivering on that promise.

It wasn't just about changing the structural operations of the company but about evolving its culture too. And you can't *evolve* a culture unless you *involve* everybody on your team.

In this chapter we'll explore the way a transformation *progresses*, and I use that word deliberately, because change isn't just about movement but about going to the next level, developing new ideas, and gaining knowledge and wisdom from each step on the path. For me, that meant finding a pace that made change possible on a large scale and figuring out how to keep the momentum going when so many different parts of our organization needed to be transformed.

During this whole time I kept asking myself, *What is the right* pace *of the transformation?* As the leader I had to orchestrate the pace so that we didn't go too fast, at a speed that our people and our organization couldn't keep up with, or too slow, which would result in missed opportunities along the way. Of course, at every step, I had some team members telling me we were going too fast while at the same time others were complaining we were going too slow.

The job of the CEO is to have a good sense of when to accelerate and when to put on the brakes. Sometimes the company is ready to move forward but the business is in the midst of its high sales season and you have to wait, or an unexpected event happens that causes you to pause. Sometimes you have a window of opportunity to accelerate and you need to seize it before the moment slips away. But one thing was always clear for me: we could not lose sight of the need for the business to meet the agreed-upon targets, to deliver results while we were in the process of transforming it.

I remember a conversation I had one day with one of the members of my team. She was concerned that things weren't happening at the kind of speed she believed was necessary. As a young executive who had worked for digital-native companies, she had understood the benefits of what we were doing, and so she was in a hurry to promote change.

Sitting in my office, she said, "Gui, your team isn't moving at the pace we need." (She was kind to say "your team" and not "you.")

I replied, "Tell me, *why* do you think we're going too slow?"

"The opportunities are clear," she said. "The vision is clear, too, as well as what we need to do next. But things aren't moving at the pace I expect them to."

"Perhaps," I suggested, "it's a question of perspective—the way you look at what's happening at our company, and the time horizon as you see it."

She obviously felt strongly and continued to press her case. "I'm looking at what we agreed to do last week, and last month, and how long it's taking to implement those decisions."

I appreciated her own sense of investment in the transformation—it's what we needed from everyone on our team—but I also realized she may not have been taking into account the many challenging factors involved in driving change in a company our size. In order to do it right, the pace may have sometimes appeared to be glacial, but that was necessary to achieve progress on such a large scale.

I said, "A few years ago we were a very successful brick-and-mortar retailer. We agreed on a new vision and a new way of working. We've decided to change the whole organization, and we're now in the process of implementing all those changes. But we're a huge organization with more than 230,000 employees, so it all takes time. When I look at what we have done in the last few years, I believe we've achieved a lot."

I could see the concern on her face. "Yes, Gui, but our competitors are also moving, and we can't afford to fall behind."

"I agree," I said. "And I'm grateful to you for sharing your perspective. We need to orchestrate it so we don't cause a disruption that's bigger than the company can cope with while at the same time we can't take so long that we lose our competitiveness. This is one of the major roles of our executive committee: to define the right pace at each moment."

That pace—and our responsibility in leadership to calibrate it—seemed to be an aspect she hadn't fully considered before. As she got up from her chair, she politely thanked me. "I'll reflect on what you just said and come back to you."

The following day, she returned to my office, saying she had given a lot of thought to our conversation and recognized the efforts we had all made and the good results we had achieved so far. I was pleased to hear that she had refined her view of what needed to be accelerated. She had begun to understand the need to strive for a fine balance between moving too fast and moving too slow, to navigate at a speed that was right for each particular phase of the transformation, given our size and objectives.

We changed speed many times. Sometimes we got it right and sometimes we got it wrong and had to change again. It was a matter of constantly listening to people, looking at what was happening in the market, and using common sense. Some people always want to accelerate while others always want to slow down. It's the leader who must make the judgment.

Often, it was the new digitally savvy hires who wanted me to make changes more quickly while it was the veteran team members who felt we needed to slow way down. I remember venting my frustration to Carlos:

"It took me a lot of time and energy to convince the more digital people to join us, and now that they're here they're getting a lot of pushback from the more experienced retailers on my team who feel the newcomers aren't considering all the ramifications of each change. They say that the younger team members aren't respecting company rules and are moving too fast to reshape a company that took the older workers years to build into a successful, trusted organization."

Carlos encouraged me to listen to both groups, to help them feel heard, and then to find common ground that was about what was best for the company. He said, "There will be times you won't make everyone happy, but that's not the job of a leader. As the CEO, you need to decide what the pace of change should be, knowing that it will need to be calibrated based on events that will sometimes be beyond your control."

The more I think about what we accomplished, the more I think of my role as being similar to that of a conductor who oversees every move of a very large orchestra. The conductor has to have a panoramic perspective, keeping the overall power of a musical work in mind while at the same time checking constantly to see and hear which individual instruments may be too loud or too soft, and when the energy and tempo of the musicians may be off. A conductor must also convey their artistic vision of a new or classic work to the board who runs the symphony and to the audiences who attend performances.

In leading an organization, the CEO is the conductor who must pay attention to the overall transformation as well as to all members of the team, orchestrating the acceptance of new members, helping newcomers adapt to the company rules, tweaking the pace of change, and selling the idea of a transformation to their bosses and associates. And, as if that is not enough, they must keep the business running smoothly and successfully the whole time.

Sometimes I tried not to think too much of all those responsibilities and to focus instead on the opportunities that lay ahead of us. Focusing on the purpose of the company played a big role in reducing my own fears and increased my motivation to promote and execute the transformation. There is nothing that stops us when we have the purpose, passion, and desire to make an impact, to bring about changes that will make a difference in people's lives.

Carlos

Gui's conductor analogy is a perfect description of how leaders set the tempo and oversee the big picture. The conductor's role is to lead a group of highly skilled musicians who are experts in their respective instruments. Similarly, Gui led a team of experts in their various functions and disciplines that made up the Walmex executive committee. Like musicians in an orchestra, they relied on his leadership to bring their best individual contributions to the collective performance of the whole company. His role required a baton that inspired, encouraged, motivated, and controlled the intensity and subtleties of the organizational rhythm as everyone moved through all changes of the transformational *partitur* (the full score).

Beginning with Beginner's Mind

Gui

As we discussed in the previous chapter, the whole process began with a mindset change. We believed we could preserve the company's clear purpose and strong values as we expanded our reach beyond traditional retail. The organization had great professionals who were experts in specific areas, and experts naturally tend to see the world from their particular area of expertise. We were asking them to make an unprecedented change, to be open to learning and seeing things differently, and we were blessed that they embraced the purpose and values of the company. With the help of Carlos, we worked together to create an environment that allowed us all to learn something new.

At one of my coaching sessions with Carlos, I told him how I was feeling encouraged by our team's transition to a new mindset. The executive committee had had a great aha moment when we linked the purpose of the company to the transformation we wanted to make. We were feeling energized and motivated to move forward and improve the lives of our customers.

Carlos replied, "You and your team have worked hard to get to the point where leaders are open to embracing the new possibilities and opportunities on the company's horizon. They're experienced and knowledgeable executives who have contributed to helping Walmex be successful."

And then he mentioned a caveat that was important. He said, "As we become experts in a particular subject or discipline, *we often lack space for ideas that do not support what we know and believe to be true and real for us.* We feel comfortable and confident operating from that 'knower' standpoint, unaware of the risk it has of limiting our curiosity for the fresh, the different, the rare, or the novel that doesn't align with our strongly held preconceptions and experiences. Psychologists use a term that relates to this, called *confirmation bias*, which refers to our tendency to process information that lines up with and supports what we believe and value."

Carlos paused to let me take in the importance of what he had just said and then asked, "Gui, are you familiar with the concept of 'beginner's mind'?"

Practicing what he has advised me to do numerous times, I said, "I've heard of it, but please tell me more."

Carlos

I explained to Gui that beginner's mind, or "shoshin," is a significant concept in Zen Buddhism. I first learned about it while reading a book about the teachings of Shunryu Suzuki titled *Zen Mind, Beginner's Mind.* The book contains transcriptions of Mr. Suzuki's talks, and in one of them he explores how the beginner's mind uses the open and enthusiastic qualities of a child's mind as a metaphor for being present, ready, and open to new things. In our case, we were helping experienced executives approach learning about the transformation without preconceptions, with the curiosity of a beginner. In other words, as a "learner" instead of a "knower."

As a quote attributed to Wei Wu Wei (a pseudonym of Terence James Stannus Gray) says, "Wise men don't judge—they seek to understand."

I told Gui it was important to be clear about this point: approaching the learning opportunities created by the changes in the business with the mindset of a beginner does not mean having to let go or dismiss our acquired experience and knowledge but rather to welcome the humility of not knowing but being eager to learn.

In other words, I explained, Gui's team and their people did not need to leave behind everything they had learned in order to lead the change. They had done important collaborative work and had come to a stage where they were ready to approach the process as a learning opportunity, not just for themselves but for the revival of the original mission of the company: *to save people money so that they can live better.*

Gui

Carlos had identified just how I felt. That my fear of changing, of losing all that I knew as I sought to reinvent myself, became a force for learning and evolving, building on what I already was so that I would be able to lead us to become something new.

I was reminded of what happened at the beginning of implementing the transformation, when we had new teams that were piloting a new way of working. When the team presented a proposal, all of us on the executive committee bombarded them with questions (see chapter 3). We were in "knower" mode, not listening with a "beginner's mind."

Carlos

It was a typical situation where senior executives, acting as experts, unintentionally turned a presentation into a challenging session, instead of using it as an opportunity for learning and growth.

I suggested to Gui that the next presentation should be more inclusive and collaborative, rather than letting the senior executives dominate it. This change would improve the outcomes of these meetings, allowing everyone present, regardless of their rank, to contribute their collective knowledge and creativity.

Gui

The day after that meeting we were discussing, one of the top leaders whom I admire a lot came to my office and said, "I totally screwed up yesterday when I questioned the team. I asked 'clever questions' and used my vast knowledge to explain my opinions and concerns, but I missed the main objective, which was to allow the team to work with data interdependently and with freedom so they would come up with different solutions for old problems that we've been unable to resolve. My 'contribution' yesterday only discouraged them and made them go back to the old way of working instead of helping them move to the new way."

I felt that what he was saying applied to all of us. We need to use our knowledge to help unlock innovation, not to block it. What we learn can give us the confidence to take risks, to experiment with the new, to pivot when necessary, or to refrain from doing something different if it has failed in the past. The wisdom we gain from experience gives us the resilience we need to continue to perform in order to transform.

Carlos

When I reflected on the complexity of Gui's role as Walmex CEO, with the multiple responsibilities involved in ensuring the success of the company and its mission, while leading a large-scale change, I recognized that one of his additional priorities was the speed of the adaptive learning process of his senior leaders. They were paid to be right and avoid mistakes, and given the command-and-control culture they evolved from, their opinions were often interpreted as orders and not as invitations to dialogue.

Therefore, Gui's leadership role as CEO included being the advocate and facilitator of their learning process. He set the example of being a humble "digital beginner" with a vigorous appetite for learning while providing experiential learning opportunities for his team. Gui helped them view the new possibilities offered by the transformation with fresh eyes and an open mind, encouraging them to evolve their emerging willingness to learn.

Making Waves

Gui

Connecting purpose and collective passion to the transformation helped us communicate the change in a much more inspirational way to our teams. I felt we were ready as a leadership team to roll out the new way of working to the whole organization. We decided that we needed to do this in waves, to start with parts of the company, to try it out, helping them learn and improve so that they'd be ready to do a rollout. This incremental process was also necessary given the fact that we were close to the end of the year and we didn't want to disrupt our biggest area, which was operations. We needed to make sure we could effectively serve our customers, to deliver on our promises during the busiest selling season of the year. Our first waves would therefore focus on the commercial side of the company.

To do it in waves was not an easy decision. Most of the companies that had done similar transformations had made sweeping changes in what is often referred to in business as "D-day." The businesses we visited explained the benefits of implementing change quickly, but because of the magnitude of our change, we made the decision to take a less disruptive, more incremental approach. This would mean having different parts of our organization working differently for months. No company of our size had accomplished a transformation in this way, but we knew it would be too much of a jolt to the organizational structure to move too fast.

If orchestrating a disparate number of moving parts had seemed daunting before, imagine the additional attention needed to drive the organization forward with some multifunctional teams going fully digital to innovate in the first waves and other groups needing to continue with the command-and-control model before migrating to the new structure in a later wave. That's when a leader is tested. I needed to be attuned to both the big picture and what was happening on a granular level. The pressure never seemed so intense, and I felt the clock ticking more than ever.

It wasn't always easy for senior leadership to let go of the way they had operated previously, to accept that our teams would tell us how to proceed. Each of the leaders had their moments of doubt, of feeling insecure, or even regressing behaviorally by reverting to old habits. We had to let go, being aware of our own filters and opening up space for learning "the new." It was a combination of delegating but not being hands off. We all had a stake in the process and responsibility for the outcome.

Two of the key leaders of the waves were Alejandra Paczka and Beatriz ("Betty") Núñez. Their insights into this transformational process will give you an idea of how we successfully used a series of waves to achieve what we called Enterprise Agility. We were literally blazing a new trail, figuring the process out as we went as there was no road map that already existed. As I mentioned, no other company our size had accomplished such a large-scale, all-encompassing transformation in waves.

Beatriz ("Betty") Alejandra Núñez Jimenez, Chief Growth Officer, Walmex

When we talk about waves, we have to go back to the initial decision point, when we had two choices—either do what's known as the Big Bang, changing a company to agile and digital overnight, or to slowly transform a company in stages. Almost all the companies we knew about had gone the Big Bang route. ING had done it, but they were a highly regulated insurance and investment company and it was necessary for them to make sure every part of their organization was on the same page, changing their structure, processes, and entire way of working in one fell swoop. But the complexity of making such an enormous change with a company our size made the Big Bang approach impossible to implement all at once. We presented our need to do it in waves to our international team and Doug McMillon, the president and CEO of Walmart, gave us his approval with only one condition: we must maintain successful results while we made the transition.

That was a big ask, but we felt we were up to the challenge. Luckily, our first wave had only 129 people. We deliberately, intentionally started small and over four months they piloted the shift—not using our traditional command-and-control model but initiating end-to-end instead.

Alejandra Paczka, Chief Talent Officer, Walmex

We started with the area of merchandising for the first wave because at Walmart merchandising is king. We felt we needed to take on this kind of challenge first to prove early on that we could get this right. A multifunctional pilot team spent four months using new methods to innovate. What was so new was that we combined different areas that usually didn't have much interaction. It was a break from doing things the old way, in silos, and it opened up dialogues for fresh ways of problem-solving that we hadn't had before.

Gui

By the time we started to see the early results from the pilot team, we were greatly encouraged: they had made impressive progress and were putting the agile methodology into practice. Multidisciplinary teams were sharing data (no one missed the silos!) as they transitioned to a fully digital operation. Even at this initial stage, we could see the potential of this new shift in mindset and way of working. If we could understand and serve our customers better and faster based on this omnichannel use of technology by a small team, the prospects of taking this transformation company-wide were exciting, bringing us swiftly and successfully into the world of e-commerce. But I understood that if we went too fast, before everyone was comfortably on board, we ran the risk of failure. Everyone needed to be 1,000% committed to this mission, without doubt or second-guessing the importance of moving forward. Rumors had already been starting to circulate that the waves would not continue and that the transformation was dead in its tracks. That kind of speculation—whether wishful thinking or not—needed to be nipped in the bud. Everyone needed to realize that we were going to proceed. Right before we were about to embark on waves two and three, we called 50 of the top leaders of the company together for a meeting. I knew this could be a make-or-break moment as I spoke with them.

I began by explaining the transformation in detail, how much we had learned from wave one, and our updated plans for the future. I saw people nodding, acknowledging the promising results yielded by the pilot team. I felt that some were sitting back like spectators at a sporting event, taking in the information but not yet totally invested. However, this was not a game but a mission, and they were not spectators but stakeholders. How to achieve buy-in on a visceral, not just intellectual, level? I reached a point in my presentation when I challenged each of them to consider their own readiness to contribute—individually—to a process that would impact the entire company and would require their own personal reinvention. In the past, the three questions had helped us define the sequence of events and link our purpose to a reason for doing it. At an earlier stage of the process, the questions had been theoretical, but now the transformation had become real, and people had seen what it was about with their own eyes. They had become very knowledgeable about what a different way of working meant. I paused for a moment, looking at the leaders sitting before me, and then I got right to the point.

"I have a special request. I want you to reflect on the three questions we've asked you previously—but this time I want each one of you to put your answers in a personal email to me. I'm looking for confirmation from each one of you that you're committed to the transformation. That you're *in*. And I want you to tell me why. Be honest in your responses. You're not helping yourself or the company to say yes when you're really feeling no. I'm prepared to be generous with anyone who disagrees with our plans and wants to leave the company."

Some nodded, a few looked taken aback, surprised by this assignment. But we were at a crucial crossroads and I wanted—no, I needed—to know that I could count on every single individual on my leadership team to make this transformation a success.

I ended by saying, "I look forward to reading your answers."

What I found fascinating was how much their responses revealed. Many wrote genuinely of their enthusiasm to be part of an innovative process. Some not only emailed me but came to see me in person. A leader knows there is a whole nonverbal language that one must know how to read in others, not just what someone says or how they say it but what their body says too. Are they leaning in to emphasize their excitement or pulling back as if they can't wait to get up and leave? Do their eyes signal an understanding of the mission and a willingness to commit to it, or a concern about what such disruptions might mean for them and even their own future career opportunities?

There were some responses that checked all the boxes and seemed to superficially say all the right things but were also somewhat perfunctory, making me question if they really wanted to make the change or would be able to, especially when change meant upending the norms they were used to. I knew that each of us would be tested by the events to come, and reality would reveal who had the dedication and resolve to withstand any of the challenges we'd face.

As it turned out, there were some who couldn't hide the fact that this wasn't what they had signed up to do. This often became clear in my personal meetings; there were a few in senior leadership who simply couldn't answer the third question: *Are you able to make the change?* It wasn't enough to know what the task was—every member of the team had to be willing and able to carry it out. To me, it became evident that there were those who disliked the notion of change, who preferred the status quo. By mutual agreement, these individuals did not stay on.

This process of asking the three questions again became a valuable way to increase motivation in others. As they expressed their own desire to be part of this mission by writing and speaking personally to me about it, they became driven to do more. I knew that once they made a firm commitment, stating enthusiastically, "I'm in," they wanted to prove it. A leader should always recognize that an exercise may have an added benefit that's not always apparent at first. The questions were not a onetime exercise, but a progressive learning experience that helped us fine-tune our preparation and to emotionally equip our team for what needed to be their evolving leadership style. As the pace of the transformation was beginning to increase, I saw the importance of bringing up the three questions again now to help people understand why they should join us at this moment *and*, by allowing everyone to determine their own resolve, it also heightened their commitment to step up to the plate to give their all. A win-win.

Carlos

This is a superb example of how Gui leads. Other leaders would be content to just use the three questions as a way to screen for readiness—not Gui. He saw in those questions a way to build motivation too. A team member who tells the CEO that they're serious about contributing to the new transformation is also giving themselves a message to live up to that commitment and be accountable. They are changing their own frame of mind. In this case, people were eager to show Gui that he could count on them to be trusted partners in the journey ahead.

Gui

Before initiating a full rollout, the team leading the change proposed cocreating the design of the new organization with a larger group of associates. This cocreation was key to not only designing the organizational changes for the waves to come, but also helped assure buy-in from all those who were charged with the implementation of the mission. They saw the higher purpose of what we were doing, which reinforced their passion to make it happen. As a larger group of associates were brought in to help design it, more of them took ownership of the process, calling it "our transformation." That was a significant benchmark. It was good for those of us who were in leadership to release power and decentralize decisions. I am sure that the new organization design was much better than the one we would have built with a few people in a closed room. If people own a mission, they will do much more to make sure we succeed.

The teams kept the focus on the problem we wanted to solve: how to be both a customer- and associate-centric company that can identify their pain points and resolve them quickly. The multifunctional teams with an end-to-end view used agile methodology, data analytics, and digital technology to discuss possible solutions, choosing one to test and learn from, and then evolving and refining it. We organized discussion sessions where we had the opportunity to understand their ideas, question some of them, debate, and decide a course of action.

Beatriz ("Betty") Alejandra Núñez Jimenez, Chief Growth Officer, Walmex

When we first began, we had our own D-day ceremony, with ribbon-cutting and a celebration to mark the start of this new system. We felt it was important to make it something special, to have this kind of exposure so everyone could witness this pilot wave being set in motion.

There was a lot of trial and error and a steep learning curve as we refined approaches, changing some of them, adding or improving others. There was an excitement that was contagious throughout the company: we could see how the team members in this first wave were really happy about their new way of working and they were productive as they concentrated on how to make the customer experience better.

Also, everyone noticed that, because of their more open agile process, the people in the first wave were able to work much faster than the rest of the company that was still doing things the old way. Others who had been doubters and naysayers (telling us that we "were killing the business") suddenly saw the positive results that were being achieved, and they began to buy in and become our strongest advocates. In fact, many of them pushed to be in the next wave, saying they wanted to be just like the pilot team—they wanted to incorporate agility and a faster-paced, digital approach into their way of working too.

When we presented our results to the international team, they were impressed—the first wave had succeeded on every metric: increasing revenue, productivity, and market share as well as demonstrating greater employee engagement and customer satisfaction. It was particularly important that our commitment to our purpose was having an impact: we were delivering more effectively to our customers.

When we asked the international team for approval to do a larger second wave, they said yes. "In fact," they said, "we want you to go bigger, bolder, and even faster!" What had happened was that now they also felt like part of the process—they were cocreating this dynamic change and felt invested in keeping the momentum going.

Our next wave encompassed 1,500 people, and once again we had a party to mark the start of it. You know, it was like having a baby shower. Just as people celebrate the birth of each child, we had a special D-day ceremony to kick off each new wave.

The magic of agility is that it not only sounds great in theory but its real-world results can be measured. Some think of it as something "warm and fuzzy," as if collaboration is just a fun new way to doing things, but it requires discipline, empowerment, and trust. You learn to focus on the process and not just the outcome. That's what leads to innovation.

But during the second wave, we noticed the teams were getting derailed. They were so in love with the process—with brainstorming new ideas and developing campaigns—that they were forgetting their main responsibility was to provide value to the customers. We quickly saw we needed to retrench and recalibrate and shift the tone.

That's when we came up with an idea that quickly turned things around: we decided to help everyone invest in the customer by presenting them with a relatable "customer persona." Using an aggregate of many different data points, we created a profile of Walmex's typical customer and we named her Andrea, a 35-year-old married mom with a baby. We had posters made featuring her and we emphasized that we needed to develop opportunities to enhance her overall experience with our company. This humanized and individualized the customer we were all working to serve. Andrea literally changed the conversation. It was a key inflection point in our focus on becoming more customer-centric. If we were going to be the ecosystem of choice for people, we had to understand their behavior, pain points, wants, and needs.

Alejandra Paczka, Chief Talent Officer, Walmex

In all, we had seven waves that converted the entire organization to Enterprise Agility. The focus of waves one and two was merchandising. Wave three encompassed supply chain, operations e-commerce, and audit; waves four and five involved all the support functions for the company; wave six was Sam's; and wave seven was omnichannel category strategy. Some departments, who were originally designated to be part of later waves, didn't want to wait. They were eager to be on the cutting edge of the transformation, to adopt the agile, digital, end-to-end approach as soon as possible.

The overall process was sometimes painful and there was some friction, some resistance. A few people found it difficult to make the transition, to take risks. They were excellent at what they did, but they weren't transformational team members.

Gui and I saw we needed to work with team members on their

behavior if we were going to change the overall culture. Of course, they needed to *want* to be part of the transformation. If they did, we had to invest the time to give them the capability to make change happen.

To shift to an agile methodology meant the teams were on a sharp learning curve. It was important for second-level managers to make decisions, to take ownership of their teams. Gui would block out time every day to walk through the office, just to learn what the teams were doing. Because people never knew when he would come to their area, they always had to be prepared, and they were. He would be encouraging and supportive, saying things like, "Oh, that's interesting. I didn't know that's how you would do this or that." All the time, *he* was learning.

When someone from one of the teams would make a presentation, Gui would ask insightful questions. For example, I remember he would constantly ask, "What's the data that supports what you tell me?" Or he would say, "We need to talk more about the customers. *What does the customer want?*" He wanted everyone to be more intentional, always putting the customer experience first.

Gui

In the end, my team and I were very proud of what we were doing as we put into action a key principle of a successful transformation: *leaders defining the what and teams defining the how.*

We were helped by the work that we had been doing with Carlos first and then with our team coach, Pedro Langre. Our team also had their own individual coaches to help bring them back to the high purpose of the change. I believe this process helped all of us reduce the size of our egos during this long, tumultuous journey.

During the implementation of the transformation, my boss Judith McKenna, president and CEO of Walmart International, suggested that I hire a mentor, a role usually played by someone more senior who has already experienced most of the issues—the doubts, uncertainties, and fears—that a younger leader faces in their career. I was already happy working with Carlos as my coach. In 2019, I hired Pedro Padierna, chairman of PepsiCo Mexico and known as a "transformative leader," as my mentor, and from our first meeting I could see the benefit of having somebody like him to advise me.

Part of the leader's job is to seek new perspectives. It's how we learn. Turn to coaches, solicit advice from mentors and other leaders. The leader who feels they know everything is doomed to fail, because they don't have the humility to acknowledge they don't know what they don't know.

As I continued working with Carlos, he pointed out that the efficacy of the transformation was directly proportional to how effectively the organization was learning. In that respect, we observed five main factors that supported the learning process involved in the waves. This is how he described them:

- *The Meaningfulness Factor:* It is crucial to ensure that the organization's leaders understand, want, and can support the value proposition and purpose of the transformation.
- *The Model Factor:* People will benefit from leaders who model an anti-bureaucratic, positive, optimistic, openly curious, and humble mindset ("beginner's mind") that will help them overcome learning biases and embrace new ideas and approaches.
- *The Learning Loop Factor:* This involves experimentation, applying what is learned, collecting feedback from customers and other relevant sources, reviewing and reflecting on key discoveries to be applied, and improving the next learning loop.
- *The Commitment Factor:* This requires everyone to fully engage in the behaviors and actions associated with the personal and collective changes needed to implement the transformation.
- *The Accountability Factor:* Each person needs to take personal responsibility for executing necessary decisions and actions that will advance the transformation process.

Carlos

It was one thing to understand conceptually what leaders needed to do, but it was a whole other thing to put the ideas into action. That's where the rubber hit the road. We did the initial work of assessing the leadership team and raising their awareness of the importance of collaboration to create enhanced capability. Now all that careful preparation was paying off.

Gui

The success of the wave approach proved to us that our early decision to take the time to orchestrate and at times recalibrate in stages was the right one. Taking it more slowly and incrementally may not have been done by an organization of our magnitude before, but we demonstrated that it could work, creating a transformation of both the company and the people dedicated to its mission. As the CEO, I may have had my own personal concerns at the beginning, but by putting my energy into constant learning and remembering the purpose we were all working toward, I was able to triumph over my fears. But as I was to find out even before we had completed the final waves, we would face a singular, devastating challenge that we never could have predicted: a global pandemic.

LEARNING POINTS FOR SUCCESSFUL LEADERS

Reinventing Yourself to Transform Your Company

Reinventing Yourself

- **Lesson:** It is possible for senior executives, who are experts in their respective fields, to unintentionally become overly skeptical when it comes to unfamiliar subjects. Their preconceived notions may hinder their ability and that of others to learn and adapt to new concepts and possibilities, which can result in delays.

> "Don't be intimidated by what you don't know."
> —Sara Blakely

- **Lesson:** To maximize learning, it's important to adopt a mindset that promotes humility, openness, and curiosity. This results in a more engaged and enthusiastic approach to learning.

"In a time of drastic change, it is the
learners who inherit the future."
—Eric Hoffer

- **Lesson:** A seasoned executive mentor can accelerate a CEO's learning and effectiveness by offering valuable and timely, content-specific guidance based on their experience, wisdom, and networks.

"A mentor is someone whose hindsight
can become your foresight."
—Anonymous

Transform Your Company

- **Lesson:** Implementing agile and digital practices in a large company can be done in waves. This allows leaders to evaluate the results and make necessary adjustments for the next wave as the organization learns, adapts, and transforms.

"Focus on constant iteration of your product
or service. Never hold too closely to your idea
but be open to change and innovation."
—Jean Chong

- **Lesson:** Just as a conductor sets the tempo for an orchestra, a CEO sets the pace for the team as they work in concert to achieve a company-wide transformation.

"A conductor needs to get into the right tempo as
quickly as possible and rectify anything that isn't right.
You need to know exactly how to get in front of the
orchestra just enough to bring them with you but not
to lose them. You have to be unflinching in showing
exactly what the tempo is even if everyone is scampering
around trying to guess and second-guess it."
—Conductor Tania Miller

8

Telling the Story

"The pessimist sees difficulty in every opportunity. The optimist sees opportunity in every difficulty."
—Winston Churchill

Gui

We can plan for all contingencies, but the future has a way of surprising us. The challenge to the transformation that none of us could have seen coming started at first with a few alarming medical reports on the news that quickly turned into a devastating pandemic that affected the world.

When COVID numbers began to precipitously rise in Mexico in March 2020, there were those who thought we should stop the transformation in its tracks. I looked at all our options. Should we stop at wave four or five? Revert back to a command-and-control model now that we were experiencing a major health crisis? If we were to move ahead with organizational change, some people would lose their jobs and new jobs would need to be created that would be very different from existing ones. Did we want to implement these disruptions as a pandemic was already disrupting so many lives?

This was one of the most difficult decisions my team and I needed to make. Ultimately, we decided we would not go back to the old way of doing things. If we postponed moving forward, we would have put at risk the jobs of many more people and delayed the creation of other jobs that were necessary to make the company stronger. As CEO I understood we were on a one-way road, and instead of reducing our speed, at this point it was better to accelerate. This was a critical time to be in the position of leading a company, to be able to see opportunities at a time when others saw only problems.

It was a challenging task. We decided to implement working from home for our Head Office associates, and what started as a precautionary measure to reduce the risk of virus transmissions became the new way of working.

We were considered an essential business by the government and so our stores remained open. While we were worried about people getting sick and dying, we also had to figure out how to make sure the company kept operating within the rules and medical guidelines, which were constantly changing, depending on the cities our stores served. At the same time, we had to keep the transformation on track, continuing our mission to adapt fully to a digital, agile organization with an end-to-end view.

This chapter is about how COVID caused us to rethink every aspect of our transformation narrative, adapting to fluctuations in real time and reshaping how we worked and lived. And within this account of how we learned to pivot, another story begins to unfold—of learning to tell the story of our mission and discovering that sometimes the act of learning to create a meaningful message for others helps *us* to understand more about the purpose of our journey. It's when we learn *how* to tell our story that we begin to realize the *why* of our story as well.

In the first few weeks of the pandemic, there was an incredible increase in panic sales as consumers were afraid of a lockdown. The fact that it was impossible to keep shelves full of merchandise only reinforced their fears and caused an uptick in their anxious buying habits. Suddenly we were processing almost two times the number of cases we had processed before. Our e-commerce business advanced *two years in just four weeks*. There was a complete shift in the days of the week our customers were visiting our stores and even the time of day they were shopping. The categories they were buying were no longer the same—for example, there was a huge increase in frozen food sales. Customers didn't like waiting in lines, fearful of contact with others, and they were concerned about people touching their merchandise. We had to start cleaning the handles of shopping carts and offer sanitizer gel at the entrance to our stores. Our cleaning measures, which had been thorough in the past, had to become even more frequent. All of this meant that we had to be more vigilant and attuned to our customers' emotional temperature on a daily basis.

Associates were working harder than ever despite their worries about their own health and whether COVID would strike their families. However, when associates were not feeling well, we needed to advise them to stay home. Ultimately, we had to temporarily replace more than 20,000 vulnerable associates with new hires. Despite the torrent of changes, we managed to keep up with all the unexpected needs. I was proud of the way we implemented safety measures to protect our customers and associates and were able to manage the crisis as it lasted much longer than we anticipated. We could make quick decisions and take fast action because we had transformed the commercial and operational areas of the company, with multidisciplinary teams doing rapid response in an agile way.

Some said we were lucky to have started on the new path we were on. The command-and-control model would never have been as effective with so many of us working remotely.

Well, the harder we worked, the luckier we got.

It was helpful that Doug McMillon, our global CEO, set very clear priorities from the beginning of the crisis. He stated that the five most important ones were: to support our associates and keep them safe; to look after our customers, helping them feel cared for and comfortable; to help others, including our suppliers; to manage the business in the short term; and to make progress in our planned strategy and even step on the gas, as the world was not going to slow down. It was a lesson that leadership matters in a crisis, and it reminded me once again of the importance of communication and defining a purpose and values with consistency and specificity.

In *The Infinite Game*, Simon Sinek says that for a business to have longevity, leaders need to see "beyond the bottom line." There needs to be a vision for sustainable growth. We could not have managed a crisis like COVID by thinking only of the bottom line. Doug McMillon and our senior leaders gave me and my team the authority and direction to play an "infinite game."

The company's response to the COVID outbreak is a story of hard choices, agile adaptability, and resilience. We had to let go of established operational procedures and to see the company—and ourselves—in a new light. As the organization evolved to accommodate new demands and a shift in customer buying habits, those of us in senior leadership had to look at ourselves and rethink entrenched patterns of our own behavior that were no longer useful in such a volatile situation. I realized that I had to change in ways that were uncomfortable at first, but that were made necessary by circumstances. It was a painful time as many in the company suffered the loss of loved ones. And it was also a time of unexpected opportunities that emerged in the midst of the crisis. We needed to be able to discern the possibilities for personal and organizational growth even when we felt lost in the fog of fear that weighed heavy on us as we confronted the destructive force of the pandemic.

Looking Backward from the Future—When the Future Is Uncertain

Gui

While we were managing the crisis, we decided to do a full review of our strategy. We knew that to succeed we needed to create our future, imagine it, and learn to look backward from it. This envisioning process was one of our key learning tools as it helped us decide what we needed to put in place now in order to get to where we wanted to go. More than 20 years before, Professor Moises Sznifer introduced me to the concept of "creating the future." According to him, many firms used to project the future based on their past, and as a result, the big determinant of their future was the past.

Other companies took a more creative approach, imagining a desired future and then constructing capabilities to reach it. Bob Johansen, Distinguished Fellow at the Institute for the Future, wrote in his 2017 book, *The New Leadership Literacies*, that it was necessary for leaders to think systematically about moving forward by looking backward from the future. "The big lesson is to be very clear about where you're going, but very flexible about how you will get there." Bob also said that while leaders in the past were expected to provide certainty, today what they need to demonstrate is clarity.

To deal with a world full of uncertainties, with everything in flux, we needed to provide clarity based on the company's purpose and values, and the direction and priorities as defined by Doug McMillon, our global CEO, and Judith McKenna, the president and CEO of Walmart International. We decided the best we could do was to create a "futures perspective" by building different scenarios and to assume the worst while we hoped for the best. At least this gave us a sense of what to focus on in the midst of constant turbulence.

We developed three workstreams, with each of these horizons having a different group of managers. There was a crisis team that dealt with urgent issues, another team to deal with opportunities that the pandemic created (such as the high demand for e-commerce), and a third team would advance our main strategic priorities.

During this time, we continued to orchestrate the pace of our transformation so we could move as one team to achieve our goal.

As the pandemic continued to take a toll and other businesses closed, a considerable number of our associates became the sole wage earners because many in their families were suddenly out of work. We made virtual visits to stores and expressed our appreciation to everyone who was working so exceptionally hard, providing them with safety equipment, training, and emotional assistance. They were on the front lines and needed to know we recognized and valued their efforts.

Learning to Improve: The Minimum Viable Person

Gui

One of the lessons I started learning before the emergence of COVID, and that was reinforced by it, was the need to experiment, to learn and improve based on the information we received. We had already achieved success applying this Learning Loop Factor to our products. Early in the transformation process we leaned into the concept of the Minimum Viable Product (MVP), with the understanding that digital-native companies had accurately read the expectations of consumers, who preferred seeing new items come to market as soon as possible, even if it meant there would be future iterations that would improve on the first version launched. It was a lesson to me in the concept of "progress, not perfection." As I mentioned in chapter 2, it was my son who first helped me to see this was the mindset of our current generation of early adopters. Over the course of the transformation, this was the method we used to bring products to market faster, refining them as we received feedback from our customers.

My own personal evolution reflected the same approach as I incrementally modified my behavior, based on feedback from my team. Carlos and I created an improvement plan, knowing that profound change doesn't happen instantaneously. It was—and *is*—an ongoing process. We tested new ways of doing things, listening to my team about how I was doing, and making adjustments as needed to keep evolving.

I had to plan to be my own MVP—no, not Most Valuable Player, but Minimum Viable Person, with noticeable improvements over previous versions of my behavior, and to keep making progress based on feedback without striving to reach some ideal of "perfection" that was unrealistic and unachievable. Carlos and my team have been my teachers in helping me learn that I was frustrating myself—and those around me—by pushing myself (and yes, those around me) to work longer and harder in the name of being *the* best. That was impossible to maintain because in life the goal posts for perfection are constantly shifting. What is the best one day becomes second-best the next. What I discovered was that I needed to concentrate on doing *my own* best, not trying to compare myself to some grand vision of ultimate perfection that would always be out of reach.

I knew I couldn't afford to slip back into old behaviors I had worked so hard with Carlos to improve. But at a time when decisions needed to be made quickly, my mind sometimes started racing a mile a minute. I knew that if people thought I was caught up in my own thoughts and not listening, that perception would override all the progress I had made. Impressions are as important as reality, and I didn't want to appear to revert back to old behaviors. Surprisingly, being on videoconference calls due to the pandemic actually enhanced my listening skills. There's an etiquette to such meetings. You have to be quiet and respectful when others are talking. If you want to speak, you have to raise your hand. You have to pay more attention to what is being said. It forced all of us to improve our ability to listen. Also, to set an example of sharing power, I handed over the leadership of our daily meeting with the executive committee to our HR leader, Eduardo de la Garza. This guaranteed that I had to follow the rules—waiting to be called on before I spoke, with no jumping in to interrupt someone else.

I realized that the same principles we were applying to transform the business were transferable to my own reinvention. Testing, learning from feedback, and improving. This was the Learning Loop Factor in action: I learned from the evolving growth of our business, and the business evolved based on my own personal growth.

The lesson here is that reinvention is reciprocal—change we experience on a human level helps to impact the way we change the company, and the way we change the company impacts the change we experience on a human level.

Carlos

Just as Gui's selected behaviors were improving, so were his team's. They were learning to cooperate and let go of their natural tendencies to resort to command-and-control mode whenever they encountered an unfamiliar situation or something that didn't align with their usual practices. For example, to implement the agile methodology, people had to manage their own feelings of being uncomfortable, vulnerable, and even fearful as they began to trust the process they were being exposed to.

Additionally, they had to hone their communication skills to speak more transparently with each other, to effectively handle differences of opinion and conflicts that were bound to arise. Trust was essential: leaders needed to demonstrate more confidence in the ability of their teams and the company to survive and eventually thrive without having to engage in the traditional, more directive style of management.

This open sharing of what we honestly think and feel in the workplace requires what Harvard Business School professor Amy Edmondson describes as "psychological safety." It is the "belief that one will not be punished or humiliated for speaking up with ideas, questions, concerns, or mistakes." That it is safe to take interpersonal risks in a group, like speaking up when one sees a problem or bringing up a sensitive issue that needs to be dealt with in order to move forward.

Gui

Simon Sinek says that "when leaders are willing to prioritize trust over performance, performance always follows," and our performance, despite the huge obstacles we were facing, was strong. We built a more effective team that started to trust others but also to have difficult conversations more frequently and in a more natural way. We could not afford to wait to make decisions or execute them.

Moment of Truth

"Self-knowledge is the root of all great storytelling."
—screenwriting lecturer Robert McKee, as quoted in *Harvard Business Review*

Gui

There is no better moment of truth than in a crisis. We worked hard to live up to our vision to be the most trusted retailer. I knew that if the transformation's purpose was to help the people of Mexico have better lives, then part of our mission during the pandemic was to put our values into practice. As a customer-centric company we felt we had to contribute to society, donating money to build a hospital and also providing food, money, and other resources to people urgently in need of them. We had not planned for any of these expenses but we understood it was the right thing to do and that our customers and associates expected it of us. We could not let them down.

In the end, the risk we took to profoundly change the organization at a time when our business had been doing well paid off in ways we could not have predicted. By starting the transformation when we did and moving forward at a pace that ensured we were bringing everyone with us, we were able to meet the demands of our people when they needed us most.

The challenge had always been to deliver great results while managing a transformation of unprecedented magnitude. We had overcome a multitude of difficulties as we got closer to reaching our end goal: a company that was digital, omnichannel, agile, and end-to-end. The enormity of this mission had brought us together, everyone working collaboratively to make it happen.

After implementing the waves in the first quarter of 2021, we felt proud of the way we had all collaborated to fulfill that higher purpose of helping the lives of so many people in Mexico.

The steps we took to move from the analog era to the digital one took all kinds of investment—financial investment in technology as well as human investment in our team and ourselves, learning to trust, pivot, and adapt. We can't drive a Ferrari if our only experience before is riding a horse. We needed to get ready for it, and to understand how to enhance our skill set and encourage others to do so to utilize technology to achieve our overall mission.

As other economies moved fast to go digital, we in Mexico benefited from being exposed to more advanced markets, and we were fortunate that our global colleagues were willing to help us. Walmex was able to learn how to design technology that would be seen by our customers as an advantage and not a threat to their lifestyle.

Carlos helped both me and my team to recognize the need for change within ourselves in order to properly change the company. This personal reinvention required a lot of effort from everyone, individually and collectively. We learned to tell others the story of the transformation by framing it as a huge opportunity to have a meaningful impact on the country, improving the lives of our customers and associates. Our effort to change was well worth it, given the size of the prize.

As we reviewed this process and started to feel comfortable with all the changes we had instituted, there was one thing that made the team uncomfortable: our perception of the lack of recognition among corporate management for what we had done to make our mission a reality. They praised us for our sales performance, but our impression was that they weren't seriously interested in what the company's massive transformation was all about. They were happy to let us proceed mainly because of our good results. It didn't feel right that there wasn't the same enthusiasm for how we had succeeded in positioning Walmex for the future.

I thought of the three questions I had asked so many people at the company years before when I was trying to determine who would be able to contribute to the transformation:

- *Do you understand the change?*
- *Do you want to make the change?*
- *Are you able to make the change?*

Although I had tremendous support and recognition from my boss Judith McKenna, I wondered if she valued as much as I did the thing we were most proud of: the transformation and the impact it would have. One day, I raised this concern with her in a Zoom conversation.

I said, "We appreciate the feedback you've given us on delivering our targets, but we haven't felt the same level of recognition for the way we've transformed the company."

Judith was curious as to how to address my concerns and replied that when the pandemic subsided, she wanted to come visit us on-site to have a full two-day immersion in how the transformed company was operating as well as how we managed to change it.

The ball was in my court. Now that Judith was giving me the chance to explain what we had achieved—in an on-site, in-person presentation—it was game on. Failure was not an option and I was feeling the pressure. Could I find the right approach to pack into two days all the changes we had made, both organizationally and in the mindset of our team?

I wrestled with what I could say that would inspire and impress my boss, to think beyond how the transformation had benefited the company financially. How could I help her see that we had engaged everyone to buy into a disruptive process, and put the mission ahead of their own career growth? What words would suffice to prove that we not only changed the company but those who were part of it too?

It was a daunting challenge. I knew I wanted to address how we had broken down silos, and Carlos had facilitated off-sites that helped everyone get to know one another better, creating an environment of trust where we could talk more freely. I needed to highlight for Judith how we had become a truly customer-centered company in the digital era. So much to say, and yet despite all the information I planned to include, it wasn't enough. Something was missing.

As I struggled to figure out what to do, my mentor Pedro Padierna and our Human Resources Senior Vice President Eduardo de la Garza suggested that we hire a professional to help me develop a clear message tailored to my boss. I resisted, thinking I had successfully done thousands of presentations in my career. *Why did I need a professional to help me put one together?* It wasn't the first or last time that I thought I didn't need help, when in fact I did.

Enter Anett Grant, who has her own company, Executive Speaking, which specializes in communication coaching for business leaders. Pedro knew her from the time he was CEO and kindly introduced us. Her methodology involves building core and satellite messages to create a narrative that will effectively engage people.

When I first called Anett, I'm sure she could hear the doubt in my voice when I explained the situation.

"I need to condense the whole story of the transformation and make it have meaning and an impact for my boss. Can you help me?"

There was a pause and then she replied, "Yes, I can. I'll help you distill your message to its essence. But I have to hear what your message is so we can convey why it matters in a concise presentation."

Anett showed me how to structure my speech and find the key message that had eluded me up to this point. She began by asking me, "What message do you want to convey to your audience and what do you want them to take away from that message?" As we brainstormed, I started to explore why I felt so passionate about taking on this all-consuming mission of changing the company. Her probing questions led to a realization that slowly emerged, and it felt like looking at the scattered pieces of a puzzle and suddenly seeing how they all fit together. She helped me tell the story of the transformation in a totally new, convincing way.

Anett Grant, CEO, Executive Speaking, Inc., executivespeaking.net

From the first time I met Gui and we chatted for two hours over Zoom, what struck me was how passionate and charismatic he is. That's a rare quality.

I work with a lot of leaders who are good, *really* good. But they're not charismatic.

With Gui, you get so engaged with what he's saying.

What I find is that many executives don't know what they want. Gui knew what he didn't want. I would listen to what he would say and then I'd craft a presentation and run it by him and he'd say, "No, that's not right. You don't understand." So I'd try again. And again, Gui would say, "No, that's not right. You gotta try again."

What it takes when working with a leader like Gui is understanding that the first few times you present the way you think he should tell the story, he's going to reject it.

I think that leaders are comfortable rejecting things. That's not a problem for them. I think the problem is for a person like me who has to create again after getting other ideas rejected.

I coach a lot of scriptwriters and I tell them they won't get a speech approved the first few tries. You just have to get something down on paper and present it, knowing they're probably going to reject it. They're going to keep rejecting different versions, but you can't take it personally. All those rejections are helping the speaker know what they really want to say. So you try another approach and another approach, and each time you and the speaker are getting closer to a final version. And then eventually you get there. You're going to go through a period of a lot of rejection and then finally it crystallizes.

It's an evolution; it's not an event.

Gui

Anett taught me that inspiration is incremental. It's not a single aha moment but grows out of all the other attempts, just like our process with the Minimum Viable Product. I understood that process.

It was Anett who opened my eyes and showed me the importance of strategically crafting a "story," approaching it from a very different angle than I ever had before. She reminded me over and over, "Tell the story, not the results." Working with her, I learned to articulate *why* what we had done had been so meaningful.

Anett

I asked Gui to take me on a tour, as if I were coming into the store like a customer, and they took me on a video tour. What struck me most was that they had a whole stack of products for only five pesos. At most other retail stores, the cheapest bag of chips is 13 pesos!

In Mexico, people have the chance to go into a beautiful Walmex store and they have the power to buy *something*. They have money in their pocket to make a purchase.

I am a pattern person so I was searching for a parallel. If we had a parallel, we could make it clear. And that's when I asked Gui to talk about the company's customer persona, Andrea.

I helped him communicate what was real, that there were millions of people like Andrea who would have opportunities that they never had before.

When I had a visual of their typical shopper, I saw that she could be a compelling parallel to the business. That's when I thought to myself, *Okay, I think I got it. I think I got what he wants.*

I told Gui, "Okay, let's do it as two stories: the customer story in parallel with the business story—the customer story, the business story."

I knew it would work because it matched the energy of Gui's delivery style.

Gui is very genuine in his vision. I was really distilling his ideas, so instead of him saying, "We're helping the people," which is such an abstraction, I helped him to use concrete, visual language so that people who didn't understand Mexico would grasp why the transformation was so powerful for an individual like Andrea. How she could become empowered. I think that's the story Gui was able to communicate.

I'm not just thinking of the words when I'm looking at a story. I'm thinking, *What does the leader need from a delivery point of view to keep the audience engaged?* Gui can get to 10,000 feet and stay there.

Gui

Anett taught me to be specific, to humanize our shopper and individualize her, showing how her story could illustrate what our company is doing to make a difference in her life.

Anett

My father was an engineer and my background was as a theater director, so I'm a theater director who thinks like an engineer.

I knew this speech would work because I had built in enough contrast: Gui could talk about the business and then get excited about talking about a typical Walmex customer. For me, a leader's presentation is all about pacing. We take down the pace and then we bring it up. It had to have a flow that was right for Gui. And he trusted me. He understood that I was giving him a way to put this exciting story into sharper focus.

It's not just managing the content and clarity elements but the delivery aspect of it too.

Gui

Anett showed me that we could talk about how our business empowered millions of individuals and that had a positive effect on our business. She thought it was really important for everyone to understand that we were delivering value and opportunities to hardworking people who shopped at our stores. That no other retailer had the scale to make that happen.

Anett

Gui is such an inspirational leader. He is very committed, and my job was to help him communicate that commitment and not get bogged down in details of the business.

Gui

It was a story of how we impact our customers and how our customers impact the business.

Anett

Once we got there, we knew it would work. It was a creative moment.

But it didn't happen until the fourth or fifth try. If you're going to tell a powerful story, you're not going to get there the first time.

Gui

Anett was persistent. She persevered.

As the country was stabilizing after the worst effects of the pandemic, my boss Judith McKenna kept her word. In the spring of 2022, people began to travel again, and she scheduled a visit to hear from us in person about what we had achieved.

Carlos

The day grew closer when Gui's boss was due to arrive. I had a coaching session with the executive committee, and I sensed that they were inadvertently viewing her lack of recognition in adversarial terms. I remember I told Gui, "Think of this as a doubles tennis match. She's not playing on the opposite team but on your team. Bring her to your side of the court and treat and involve her as part of the team. I'm sure she wants to see you win."

Gui

Carlos was right. We all had the same goal. My boss Judith always supported me and our business. She had a great way of challenging and encouraging us, which helped us to move faster and discover ways to improve the organization. She inspired us to be better. Knowing she would be coming to see us in person made me hopeful that we could show her why we were so excited about what we had done. It also sent the message to us that she was seriously invested in hearing what we had to say. That kind of response was an excellent motivator for us. I began to wonder if, perhaps, it was the fact that COVID had kept us all separated that had played a major role in preventing her from fully understanding our accomplishments. Having Judith engage in face-to-face conversations with me, my team, and our associates would make a big difference.

The Trial Run

Gui

Before delivering my presentation in front of Judith McKenna, I did a trial run for input before the whole executive committee. As I spoke, I found myself getting emotional. "With this transformation, we can provide access to a whole new world to our customers, the world of the digital economy. They didn't have the internet so they couldn't schedule a telemedicine appointment. They didn't have bank accounts, or the means to visit a doctor. But our transformation now gives us the platform to connect our customers with service providers. We're able to negotiate a price on their behalf so they can afford the internet. And we are dramatically reducing the acquisition costs for those digital companies. We have a unique opportunity to improve the lives of our customers beyond traditional retail, and we're already starting to offer them internet and phone services at one-third the price they used to pay."

I added, "And the internet is just the beginning. The digital world also offers a wealth of essential services and products, like telemedicine, bank accounts, education, social media, and e-commerce. If people aren't connected to that world, either because they can't afford the internet or they don't have a payment method to purchase all those services and products, how can they benefit from the digital revolution?"

As I looked around the room, I saw the way people were taking in what I had said, and I knew I had begun to reach them in ways that I hadn't before. I finished by saying, "I love Walmart's purpose and I find myself in a situation where, by doing what I love to do, I can help millions of people."

When I was done speaking, I saw that everybody was emotionally engaged; some were even wiping tears from their eyes. We had a unique opportunity to do good and do it well.

In my presentation, I successfully found the elusive aha moment I had been looking for. For too long we had been using defensive arguments to promote the transformation: that we needed to defend ourselves against digital-native companies and start-up players. But framing the mission in aspirational terms, as a way of improving the lives of millions of our Mexican customers and their families, provided the personal and collective motivation that gave the transformation deeper meaning. We were doing it for a purpose that was bigger than ourselves, and that gave us a new sense of commitment.

Our founder built this company to help people save money and live better. Now that we had completed the transformation, we would be able to radically grow our capacity to serve our customers and would be a tremendous vehicle to improve their lives. That was the glue we needed to have.

Before this, I had related purpose only to the company, but while working with Anett I connected the dots, linking purpose to the transformation itself. That's when I realized that the changes we had been making were just a means to an end, which was to do something meaningful that had an all-encompassing impact. It was clear that our customers' needs would not be resolved by the physical world: a bank would not open an account for them because many of them would not be "profitable customers," and a doctor's office would not schedule a visit for those of our customers who didn't have insurance or funds to pay for it. But we could give them access to the digital world at a price they could afford, making opportunities (like financial credit and telemedicine) available that they otherwise would not have access to. Just as our stores offered products to our customers at a low price point, we could now also open new doors to them, making must-have services available that were off-limits before.

If the transformation had failed, we would have failed so many of the families we saw every day, the friends and neighbors, old and young, *las mamás*, *los papas, los abuelitos . . . las familias.* The community we served was not an abstract concept, but real people with hope in their eyes. Their dreams were the reason we were driven to succeed.

D-Day

Gui

The morning I was set to present to my boss Judith McKenna, I kept reminding myself, *Tell the story, not the results.* I would start the day with an overview of the transformation and then members of my team would make individual presentations to her, drilling down on the specifics.

I felt confident. I wouldn't be delivering a long, numbers-driven presentation but a short talk that would hopefully impress Judith and help her appreciate the full scope of our mission. My team and I had worked to build the story, training with Anett to constantly pare our presentations to their essence. I knew that just because I had a successful trial run didn't mean that I was sure to hit it out of the park this time.

I realized that our narrative was never really about bottom-line numbers or defending ourselves against our new digital competitors, but about the passion and purpose behind what we had done. I needed to convey the impact of the transformation so it would resonate on an emotional level with Judith.

I took a deep breath and told the story of our transformation, emphasizing the impact it had on our customers—so many people were being lifted up by our new way of working. I spoke at length about the purpose of our mission and how it aligned with the core values of the company.

What we had accomplished wasn't helping an abstract population. It was changing the lives of people who were just like our customer persona. Not only would she be able to shop our much bigger online catalog using her computer or mobile phone, but we could help her afford Wi-Fi, to complete her college education, to see the doctors she needed and have her prescriptions filled, and to sign up for a credit card and other banking services at a fraction of the cost she'd typically have to pay. All because everyone at Walmex had worked together to achieve a transformation that no other company our size had accomplished before. This transformation would be honoring the customer-centric values of our founder and we'd be doing it on a grand scale through digital technology and agile methodology that would allow us to succeed as the country's most trusted retailer in the future.

When I was done with my speech, I could tell my boss Judith had a deeper understanding of why the transformation mattered so much, and she expressed her appreciation and support in a way that made us all feel a sense of pride. It was only after telling the story that my team and I understood better what we had done—we finally connected the dots.

I could tell that everyone in attendance that day got the importance of what we had done. Though Anett had emphasized the importance of keeping my presentation short—under 10 minutes—that was a challenge I wasn't able to meet. However, I managed to convey the story of the transformation in a structured way, which was a major feat for me! This was a powerful experience, and the reaction from Judith reenergized everyone in the company.

At the end of the day Judith was very pleased with what she saw, and I realized that she actually knew much more about the transformation than we had thought. She told us how much she appreciated what we had accomplished and said that on the following day she wanted to openly discuss our sentiment that we had not been adequately recognized for our efforts. She asked us to think about the reasons overnight, so we'd be able to answer her question, "Why do you think I didn't recognize you for all that you had done?"

A Question and an Epiphany

Gui

That was the question that kept running through my mind as I arrived home. *Why did we think she hadn't recognized us for all that we had done?*

I began to reflect on my coaching sessions with Carlos, where I wasn't receptive to the feedback from my team until he helped me to truly recognize the value of listening to them. Was I having the same response now, simply playing the victim instead of being open to what my boss's question was telling me? It occurred to me that perhaps the root of the issue was on my end of the table. And then a realization struck me: if the audience is not able to comprehend the message, it's often due to *shortcomings in the communicator's delivery.*

I realized that even though we had broken down silos in our organization, my team and I had been viewing the transformation, and updating my boss on its progress, as a discrete series of advances, "silos" of successful changes:

- The change to digital capabilities
- The change to agile methodology
- The change to MVP development
- The change to involving suppliers and customers in some of our innovation projects
- The change to seeing opportunities to launch new verticals

In the past I had talked about these accomplishments as separate victories, outlining "the what," and my team had filled in "the how," but we had never really explained "the why" to my boss, Judith. How could she have known why the transformation meant so much to us? It wasn't just that we had changed our way of working that mattered the most. Or that we had been the only company our size to implement such a massive change. We were looking at our own story in fragmented terms instead of seeing that the sum of these parts served a higher purpose. But this time we had conveyed our story of transformation in terms of interdependent connectivity, spokes that were all related to a central hub—the core values that were the driving force of our company and added value to our customers' lives.

That higher purpose had been a strong source of motivation for our associates. The mission was the message and it inspired my team to fulfill the transformation's larger purpose. It also helped me recruit more new hires, especially young people who were not only interested in succeeding but in finding work that was meaningful too. They wanted to help improve people's lives and now we were giving them the opportunity to do that in a bigger way.

The answer to Judith's question had been staring me in the face, but I hadn't been able to see it before now.

Day Two

Gui

The next day, when Judith brought up again the subject of why we felt she hadn't been supportive of our efforts, my team looked at me, expecting that I would express the reasons for our long-simmering frustration. There was a hush in the room.

With all eyes on me, I said, "I believe that the recognition we had been expecting from you did not happen because we hadn't properly told our story to you. And I think that's because we weren't ready to tell it yet."

No one was more surprised I said this than me. Not because I was taking responsibility—I believe it's the leader's job to be accountable when necessary—but because everyone had always praised me as an excellent storyteller. I prided myself on that ability. I used stories to share experiences, to help others learn, and, in particular, to persuade people to consider different perspectives. Storytelling is very natural for me; you might say it's in my comfort zone. It was this quality, coupled with my passion for work, that led people on my team to speak of the "Gui Factor."

Because storytelling was something I thought I knew how to do well, I didn't expect that the one place I had come up short was in telling the story of the transformation. But my learning loop was to discover once again that the tools I thought I had mastered did not serve me in every situation. I was not as ready as I thought I was.

I had relied too much on highlighting operational achievements without showing that they were simply the means to a much more meaningful end having to do with helping others.

It amazed me that we hadn't been able to connect all the dots when we first built the plan, but it dawned on me that this is how things work—you have a vision, you start working on it, but the picture is never complete from day one.

You never have the full story until you've lived it and made improvements and adjustments to the initial inspiration, refining, revising, and gaining clarity on what it means. Until you have the full story and understand it, how can you put it into words that will have an impact on others? It's an ongoing learning process that takes time.

My boss Judith was so impressed with the way I had told the story of our transformation that she asked me to give the presentation to the company's global CEO Doug McMillon and the chairman of the board. But there was one caveat:

"You'll need to tell your story in a compelling way in just three minutes when you deliver it for them. Anything over that is too long."

At first, I did not take Judith seriously. *Three minutes?* To me, this was an impossible task. I like to talk, and since I felt especially passionate about this subject, I had a lot to say.

While I never was able to condense my presentation to only three minutes, I did succeed well enough to be invited to tell the story of the transformation to the entire Strategy Committee of the Global Walmart Board.

Carlos

In an August 18, 2022, BBC article, author Kate Morgan reveals that a high percentage of people "want their work to have meaning." She quotes Aaron De Smet, a senior partner at McKinsey, who said the Industrial Revolution was responsible for work becoming "transactional." She then cites a 2018 survey of American professionals, which found that "nine out of ten workers would trade a percentage of their earnings for work that felt more meaningful." She later adds, "In an analysis of workers across half a dozen countries, De Smet and his colleagues found that nearly 90 percent of workers between the ages of eighteen and twenty-five said having a positive societal and environmental impact in their career was very high on their list of priorities." Gui was tapping into that very desire among the people on his team. He took what was personal for him and showed how it could be universal, reinforcing the benefits of the transformation, and changing the very way his colleagues perceived it.

The Magic of Storytelling

"People do not buy goods and services. They
buy relations, stories, and magic."
—Seth Godin

Carlos

In his newsletter *In Pursuit of Elevation*, Be-Cause LLC founder and CEO Mats Lederhausen writes that Yuval Noah Harari, the best-selling author of *Sapiens*, "has studied thousands of years of human evolution and is very clear in his view that humans are basically storytellers. In fact, he asserts that our capacity for storytelling is what has enabled human evolution and progress."

Those of us who coach leaders are familiar with the benefits of framing achievements in terms of the compelling story behind them. The business world sees how literature, theater, and film have something valuable to teach us about constructing a narrative that will engage others. In fact, *Harvard Business Review* interviewed Robert McKee, "the world's best-known and most respected screenwriting lecturer," who told them, "A big part of a CEO's job is to motivate people to reach certain goals. To do that, he or she must engage their emotions, and the key to their hearts is story . . . In a story, you not only weave a lot of information into the telling but you also arouse your listener's emotions and energy."

Executive leadership coaching often reveals the power of storytelling. During leadership assessments and stakeholder interviews, data is collected and analyzed, and what emerges is a story. In our case, the narrative revolves around Gui, the CEO who is eager to implement changes and innovations in the company's operations. The cast of executive leaders has differing levels of enthusiasm about his ideas, and some have concerns about his leadership behaviors. As Gui's coach, my job was to weave all the data collected into a meaningful, believable, and motivational story.

Gui

The story became clearer each time my team and I told it, and as part of our ongoing work, we did follow-up presentations to show the progress we were making. Carlos had instilled in me the importance of following up, and I learned how much credibility you get when you deliver on your promises. It was not only about looking backward from the future but building toward it in the here and now.

In one presentation, I addressed 1,000 of our employees in person and another 5,000 by video, and as I shared the story of the transformation I witnessed how they became even more motivated when they understood that the link between our purpose to change people's lives and our mission gave us a new ability to do more for our customers. Our investors who heard the speech were also excited about the potential growth ahead of us. All due to the power of the story.

When I presented to one of our top suppliers, they wanted to transform their company just as we had done. The ripple effect, as change inspires change, has been amazing to see.

Sometimes I have expanded on my own telling of the story by asking associates from our stores to tell their own stories in their own words about how the transformation has personally benefited them. One middle-aged female associate said that she signed up for the education membership we offer and was going back to school to earn her degree as an example to her kids. She revealed that her life has changed because of the ways we can now help our customers and associates to enhance all facets of their lives. I could talk about the transformation succeeding because we all believed in the higher purpose behind it, but my story was made even more significant by the individual stories of our associates.

Communication is even more powerful when you can provide evidence that you are putting into practice what you're talking about in your story. As my boss Judith kept saying, "One for saying and nine for doing." Every time we told the story to different groups, we were able to point to information about a new pilot program we had in development or that showed our customers were buying at higher rates from us using e-commerce or our prepaid mobile phone service.

Another benefit of sharing the story: when we survey our associates, their responses reveal a high level of engagement with the company that few of our competitors can match with their employees.

Carlos

The ability to tell a story is a powerful device in the leadership toolbox.

In the Walmex transformation story, Gui's use of this tool has been a crucial element of his leadership. At the start of the process, the comparison between new digital start-ups and once-successful companies that were lagging behind, becoming "dinosaurs" about to go extinct, was a powerful metaphor. It influenced, inspired, and engaged the entire organization. Gui made it relatable by highlighting that he didn't want to suffer the same fate. This helped establish a connection to the journey they were all about to embark upon.

An important aspect of effective leadership consists of creating opportunities in the minds of team members. Telling a compelling story helps to illustrate and humanize ideas in a logical, vivid manner, using anecdotes, emotions, and imagery that can be felt at an intellectual and emotional level. It's a potent technique to capture the interest and backing of your collaborators.

As Joseph Campbell, the author of *The Power of Myth*, once said, "People forget facts, but they remember stories."

Leadership often employs storytelling as a tool to influence their employees in the organization. However, as we have seen here, it is equally important to recognize the potential of a cohesive and well-delivered story to make a significant impact in an upward direction. By acknowledging the influence and contributions of senior leadership, a shared sense of purpose and alignment with the organization's values and mission can be strengthened.

Developing a story that supports the common humanity and values of all those in pursuit of organizational success is a critical leadership task.

Recognizing Those Who Make a Difference

Gui

Even before speaking to my boss Judith about being recognized for the transformation, the idea of giving credit to others was something I took seriously. I knew what it felt like to seek validation, and I understood this was at the core of our humanity—wanting to be seen for who we are, and acknowledged when we go beyond the call of duty. Judith instituted an award to honor people in the company for their special achievements and this was not something I was going to outsource. I wanted to meet with each person we selected for this award, to look them in the eye and thank them personally for making a difference. These meetings were as emotional for me as they were for the people we were honoring. I was able to learn about and recognize many successful stories, showing the whole organization how important it was to appreciate those among us who had made a difference.

Eduardo de la Garza, Chief Human Resources Officer, Walmex

Gui is an innovative, enthusiastic dreamer who puts the customers and associates at the center of everything we do. He obviously recognizes his commitment to deliver the business results agreed upon with the organization, but at the same time he is vehement about looking out and caring for our people and their development.

There are things Gui does not want to delegate, and one of them is giving recognition to others. For example, we have what we call the "Make a Difference Award," which is given to directors, managers, and associates for going the extra mile in some way. While it comes with monetary recognition, this award is treasured because it identifies those employees who have made a difference, not just to the success of Walmex, but to the lives of others.

Over a year's time we have given awards to 120 people in the company. Gui takes five minutes to personally sit with every one of these recipients, to acknowledge and recognize their commitment to making a difference and explain why this award is being given to them. And believe me, the excitement that he generates throughout the company is incredible. To have a few minutes with the CEO of the company really impacts people at a deep emotional level. He honored one of our colleagues in HR about three months ago, and ever since, the energy she brings to her work is amazing.

Each year we receive about 1,800 proposals, and after screening through all of them, we come up with 300 proposals that Gui reviews personally. He takes this as seriously as any of his other responsibilities. I was sitting with him once going over a proposal, which showed that the person being considered had an exemplary performance record. Gui responded that a promotion for the employee was already in place.

"What else is there that makes him deserving of this award?" he asked.

"His store has contributed substantially to our bottom line."

"What else?"

One of the other people at the meeting spoke up. "There was a shooting at his particular store and in that moment of crisis he acted quickly to protect the customers trapped in the store, giving more than one hundred people food and blankets for the twelve to fourteen hours they were there."

Gui nodded solemnly and said, "He will get an award." I could see how these details had moved him and it once again showed me how Gui's priorities were about something that transcended the usual transactional nature of business. For him, it was about people who invested their time and efforts in others.

For recipients who come to his office to receive this recognition, it's an experience they never forget.

As he handed the award to the man who had helped so many during the crisis at his store, Gui said, "You are here because you make us proud. Without you the company would not be who we are."

When a recipient cries at being told by the CEO of the company that they are deserving of such a recognition, Gui cries with them.

Gui inspires me because he is a leader who goes the "extra mile."

LEARNING POINTS FOR SUCCESSFUL LEADERS

Reinventing Yourself to Transform Your Company

Reinventing Yourself

- **Lesson:** A good story helps us not only grasp the message intellectually, but it also strikes emotional chords in us that can move us to take action. It's also more memorable than a dry, factual presentation.

> "Stories have power. They delight, enchant, touch,
> teach, recall, inspire, motivate, challenge. They help
> us understand. They imprint a picture on our minds.
> Consequently, stories often pack more punch than sermons.
> Want to make a point or raise an issue? Tell a story."
> —Janet Litherland

- **Lesson:** Reinvention is reciprocal: the best way to transform your business is to transform yourself too.

> "People who cannot invent and reinvent themselves
> must be content with borrowed postures, secondhand
> ideas, fitting in instead of standing out."
> —Warren Bennis

- **Lesson:** If you feel you and your team aren't receiving proper credit from your boss, first consider if you have clearly communicated the reasons why you deserve that recognition.

> "If we don't communicate, we certainly can't
> get much done and if we don't communicate
> authentically, what we get done is less effective."
> —Michele Jennae

- **Lesson:** When you need to deliver a presentation, reach out to those who can coach you to effectively deliver your message.

> "I have been fortunate to have some amazing
> coaches and mentors who have helped
> me become the player I am today."
> —Lionel Messi

- **Lesson:** Consistent messages that recognize and appreciate the work of your team will foster gratitude, belonging, and a sense that they are contributing to the success of the company.

> "Recognition is not a scarce resource. You
> can't use it up or run out of it."
> —Susan M. Heathfield

Transform Your Company

- **Lesson:** Tell the story, not the results.

> "Stories that surface optimism in the face of adversity
> are not naiveté. They are a way to look at possibilities
> rather than foregone conclusions. If you craft a narrative
> that includes a context of the way things were as well
> as the way things can be, you provide a road map to
> make sense of the world in ways that inspire hope."
> —John Baldoni

- **Lesson:** Change we experience on a human level helps to impact the way we change the company, and the way we change the company impacts the change we experience on a human level.

> "Reinvent your business constantly. The end goal may be the
> same, but the tools and methods are constantly evolving."
> —Ken Tucker

9

The Path to Optimal Leadership

"Earn your leadership every day."
—Michael Jordan

Gui

The implementation of the waves in the first quarter of 2021 did not mean the end of the transformation but was actually a whole new beginning for the company, just as a graduation is often called a commencement. Because of the journey we had taken—both individually and collectively—we had changed in ways we could not have predicted.

This chapter is about the aftermath of the transformation and how the company and I had learned to evolve. I became a better leader by listening more effectively to my team, and Walmex became an even better company by listening more effectively to its customers. The results of the transformation were manifold: we created new benefits for customers that went far beyond the retail experience, enhancing more facets of their lives. Listening leads to learning, which then leads to turning points that resolve pain points.

As the major implementation phase was completed, we realized that a transformation never ends; it just takes pauses. New opportunities arise as more exciting advances in technology develop. New possibilities emerge as we find more expansive ways to understand our customers and how to meet their needs.

Leaders should see their company's transformation as a constantly unfolding story, just as their own lives unfold over time.

The Leader as Architect of Meaning

"The leader's role is to make sense of things for their
culture. This is the leader as Chief Sense-Maker."
—Jay Steven Levin

Gui

A CEO must never lose sight of the company's core values, even during times of enormous change. It is crucial to align the mission with a higher purpose that will energize and motivate everyone on your team. In this way, the leader becomes the architect of meaning, constructing a message for the mission ahead. Just as an architect designs the blueprint for a house so that it will withstand the test of time, making sure the foundation is solid enough to support it, a leader must envision a structural framework for the transformation that is built on a goal that will endure despite all the turbulent disruptions that will inevitably occur.

Many make the mistake of thinking that achieving a better bottom line or gaining a competitive edge will be all that's needed to fortify the scaffolding of the process. But that kind of mindset is never enough to carry out a plan with the passion of purpose that's required. The meaning must go beyond a company's self-interest and instead be rooted in a visceral sense of benefiting others. Of going beyond the call of duty to become a different kind of calling, one that causes everyone to be stakeholders in a cause that resonates with them emotionally and not just intellectually.

The charge of an architect is to summon a substantial structure into being, to be a visionary who can take an idea that exists in their imagination, and using practical tools, help it take shape—first on the page and then bringing it to life as a building that will become part of the landscape and the community, a place for people to make their own, whether it's a house, a sanctuary, or where the business of the day is done. A leader, like an architect, must be a dreamer first·

who can develop a purpose that will meet the needs of their team, inspiring them to want to be part of their vision for the future.

Carlos

Architects consider the relationship between physical space and spatial design as they create amazing structures that will evoke special emotions in us as we experience them. Similarly, leaders understand the impact of the social and psychological contexts they must manage to bring out the best in their team. One of the crucial abilities of leaders is to discern what will be meaningful to the people they need to motivate. They must take a mission that may read like nice words on a wall plaque and transform it into something that touches the hearts and minds of others, giving them a compelling reason to work toward it.

Gui

There is a phrase that "the personal is universal," but I believe the opposite is also true—"the universal is personal." Whatever code of values or purpose is driving your company must also have deep resonance for every person you're working with. They have to make that meaning their own so that it informs their individual motivation as well as one that's collective. For a transformation of a company to be successful on a large scale, it must be the accumulation of many transformations that occur on a human scale—changes big and small that turn employees into stakeholders who are invested in the overall vision. A leader defines the mission's primary meaning, and it's every member of the team who identifies a private meaning that will influence the actions they take.

In my career I met somebody who had great insights, but she often second-guessed her own ideas. That led to her being hesitant to make decisions. She excelled at problem-solving, but the one problem she had difficulty solving was how to *not* get in her own way. Eventually, she joined a networking group of senior women executives from other companies who met on a regular basis to support one another in the corporate world. When she saw that she could be an inspiring role model to others in the group, this gave her the incentive to conquer her fears and become more decisive. She also became a more valuable member of our team as we transformed the company. She discovered a personal purpose to help us accomplish the universal one.

As the CEO of the company, I couldn't always know what each person's individual purpose might be. There were times I could see where they needed to make improvements and I'd suggest ways for them to change their behavior, but ultimately that decision was up to them. A leader is responsible for the big-picture meaning that must be the engine that motivates the team as a whole. Finding the right purpose that will stimulate others is what finally determines the success of any transformation. Ultimately, that's what this book is all about.

In our case, the purpose was already defined long ago by our founder, and it continues to be aligned with what the company does today and wants to do in the future. I felt it was also very much aligned with my own goals. My objective was to energize people by linking our purpose with our strategy and to let them see the impact we could have on people's lives.

Walmex evolved because those of us within the company evolved. We began to view our customers in 360-degree terms—expanding our efforts as a retailer to enhance their daily experience with resources such as Wi-Fi, banking, education, and health care. Just as we had broken through the silos that had limited the ways we interacted within the organization, we also broke through our siloed mindset when we considered how to use technology to benefit our customers in more all-encompassing ways.

As we saw our customers as individuals who had many facets to their lives, we could ask ourselves questions we had not asked ourselves before: *What are their needs outside of Walmart that are going unmet? Can we help them achieve their goals in a multitude of areas?* We were thinking way outside the box and finding that by addressing our customers holistically we were also building up their loyalty to the Walmart brand online and in our brick-and-mortar stores.

They understood we were making them our number-one priority and that's why they chose us, even as new competitors were trying to capture market share. The transformation was never solely about using technology for its own sake but for the sake of our customers and associates. As we increased our technological tools and expertise, we also expanded our perspective on how we could service the people who depended on us.

As I mentioned in a previous chapter, I had seen other companies stray from their original core values and lose their way; we went the opposite direction, emphasizing what made our company a trusted brand in the first place.

We utilized technology to provide us with more data points, but we never lost sight of the human factor: we became digital not just to do things faster but to serve our customers better.

Leadership Is Not a Job, It's a Way of Being

Gui

This chapter sums up a number of the lessons we have covered throughout the book and adds a few new ones as well. In different ways this has been a story of character—the essential qualities a leader brings to a mission so that the end goal can be effectively achieved. Hard work and skill are important, but they should be expected of anyone in any position. What I'm talking about here are those aspects that speak to an individual's deepest instincts, the very nature of their humanity: honesty, integrity, authenticity, humility, determination, and generosity. Too often these are merely buzzwords that aren't put into practice. But without these fundamental ingredients, there is no foundation to reinforce and support a leader's vision as they steer the company in new directions.

I never think of being a CEO as simply "doing a job"—for me, leadership is a way of being that draws on everything I have experienced and learned throughout the course of my career. We mustn't fall into the trap of putting these qualities into silos, with honesty separate from humility or authenticity put in one box while generosity resides in another. We can't compartmentalize these attributes any more than we should subdivide our soul. Who we are as leaders is the sum of all we have experienced. When I was looking at all the ways to change the company, I kept seeing parallels between how a company can run most effectively and how a leader can achieve a peak level of performance. Both need to be adaptable and learn from mistakes; to reach their full potential, both need to move away from a command-and-control approach to one that's more multifunctional and omnichannel. Just as a company should serve its customers, a CEO should be a servant leader, listening to a diversity of opinions and encouraging decision-making among team members.

There is a saying that God gave us two ears and one mouth so we could hear more than we talk. How many times have we refused to listen to what people were telling us? How many times did we believe that we had the answer, so why bother to listen to what others had to say? We have written at length about the art of telling a story, but as one leader once said, "Unfortunately, when people become leaders, they spend more time telling stories than listening to stories." While there is great value in knowing how to create a narrative that will win hearts and minds, we must never forget to open our own hearts and minds to the stories of others.

As we were reimagining what Walmex could be, I found myself rethinking what I could be too. With Carlos's help and the advice of my trusted mentors, I realized that evolution occurs on many levels, within a company's structure and operations as well as within the people who are responsible for the organization's success. Change is the constant in all things, and what helps a company grow is similar to what helps us grow as human beings: a recognition that growth is not only possible but necessary. It's not enough to set a corporate transformation into motion without personal reinvention too.

Carlos

Improving your leadership skills within a specific organization can be a challenging task. It is crucial to identify negative behaviors and attitudes that could potentially hinder your growth as a leader. Often, these behaviors become so ingrained that they may seem like an inherent part of your identity, and you may not have even realized that they are problematic. It is essential to be willing to accept feedback from others and consider the potential drawbacks of ignoring it. This feedback can provide valuable learning opportunities, helping you grow and evolve as a leader. To change these behaviors, you need to be honest, open, and courageous, willing to step out of your comfort zone and adopt new behaviors that can make you a more effective leader. However, an insecure person may view constructive criticism as an attack on their credibility and ability to lead others, instead of seeing it as a valuable tool to help them grow.

Most of us expect leaders to be self-confident. Imagine if you were on a plane and heard the pilot voice their anxieties about flying. It would be a bumpy ride in more ways than one. Still, even CEOs who are secure in their leadership abilities may struggle with doubt. The key is to find a balance of the two so that we don't grow overly confident to the point of arrogance but neither do we get so insecure that we become paralyzed by fear or self-doubt.

It's more common for CEOs who are at the top of their game to tip the balance toward arrogance. They've far exceeded expectations in the past and they're sure they'll do so again. They even quote Shakespeare, saying, "What's past is prologue." And while it's true that history often does repeat itself, when a leader becomes too self-confident, they lose perspective about how they actually reached a certain pinnacle of success, forgetting that they listened to others on the way up and not just themselves. Suddenly, they begin to tune out colleagues who voice opposing points of view.

Despite all the wonderful and well-deserved positive feelings brought about by success, if we don't manage them properly it can also bring about an illusion of infallibility. This is one of the factors that can lead to arrogant behaviors, which keep us from listening and considering potentially better alternatives, which in turn may sabotage the continuous learning that the organization must sustain in order to maintain what it has achieved. I believe that a fundamental piece of the transformation puzzle must be strengthening the company's character traits, in much the same way that leaders must refine and improve their own behavior.

Gui

A CEO must make difficult decisions every day. You have to look at the data that's available and listen to as many people as possible in order to take calculated risks. But, in the end, you are the ultimate decision-maker. If you are concerned about what the "correct" decision is, you may not act quickly enough, and any delay could cause you to lose ground to your competitors. On the other hand, if you make uninformed decisions and act rashly, you could end up putting the company in danger—and probably lose your job.

If your first intention is to please people and be seen as a "good" person, you will fail to make choices that are right for the company but may not make everybody happy. The fact is a leader who tries to please everyone is setting themselves up for failure—for they'll find they're not pleasing anyone at all. You have to come to terms with the fact that some people will disagree with you and express their disappointment in you, but if you want to be well liked all the time, you shouldn't aspire to be a CEO.

One night after a challenging day at work, I shared with my wife, Patricia, that I felt people were judging me too harshly about a critical decision I had made.

I told her, "I've been working hard to improve myself by becoming more attentive to others and keeping my cool even during challenging situations. But despite my best efforts, there are still members of my team who aren't satisfied. And I get frustrated that they don't understand *my* perspective. They disagree with me when I make difficult decisions."

Patricia responded by saying, "I don't see it as a problem that some people don't agree with you. Why do you expect that they should when you know that's not always possible?"

"But it's unfair," I insisted. "My intentions were good, and I had thought long and hard about what needed to be done. They should understand why I made this decision and give me their full support."

I could tell Patricia was not going to give me her support either. She quickly replied, "Now, you just sound arrogant, portraying yourself as the victim in this situation."

"Me? Why do you say that?"

"Because it's true. Even the most admired leaders in history don't please everybody, so why do you think you're the exception to the rule? Don't set unrealistic expectations for yourself."

"Are you turning against me too?"

"Of course not," she said with a sigh. "I know you're always trying to do your best for the business. And you've created an environment where people feel safe to express their opinions so you can see a problem from many different angles. You yourself have said that a diversity of opinion helps the team make better decisions."

"It does, but after listening to everyone, I want them to back me up when I decide on a strategy." I explained that I feared that the ones who weren't on board with me may be less efficient when it came time to implement the decision.

"Did they fight you on it?" she asked.

"No," I said. "They just didn't look happy."

The silence from Patricia that followed gave me my answer. It didn't matter that they weren't happy. The important thing was that they accepted what I had decided, no matter how they personally felt about it. Patricia saw clearly that I was falling into the trap of being arrogant, expecting total agreement just because I was the CEO. The fact that they could let me know they were displeased was a signal that we had a work environment where it was understood that critical feedback could be expressed, even to the boss. They knew there would not be repercussions for how they felt about my decision.

As a leader I had to be willing to acknowledge that my team was composed of knowledgeable, innovative professionals who would be honest with me and that I was lucky that they sometimes disagreed with me. I wanted individuals who were opinionated and felt free to say what they thought. I was getting upset by the very thing that I prized about my team. I had to admit my wife was right—I was needlessly playing the victim, letting arrogance get the best of me.

Carlos

I remember discussing this with Gui and telling him I agreed with Patricia. At one of our initial team off-sites, we explained that it's important for everyone's point of view to be properly heard and considered, even when some don't agree at first with a decision. But this must not be confused with needing to have a consensus. Once a decision has been reached, the team must walk away from the meeting committed to working together to make it happen. As the great Chicago Bulls coach Phil Jackson once said, "Good teams end up being great teams when their members trust one another enough to renounce their 'me' in favor of their 'we.'"

One of the primary flaws of the arrogant leader is that they don't listen or believe they must change. Even when they gain short-term results, they usually will not be successful in the long term. The central idea of this book is the importance of connecting the process of change with a strong and meaningful purpose in a way that inspires leaders and the organizations they run to work collectively to achieve a higher goal. To be effective, they must be open to change and adapt their behavior as they go through the sometimes painful process of discovery and transformation.

Gui

Well, it's one thing to get challenging feedback from coworkers, but another to get it from your wife. Still, I admit, in both cases, it pays to listen closely!

The Cost of Complacency

Gui

Another threat to strong leadership is allowing yourself or your team to feel so secure in the success that's been achieved that you begin to become complacent. When people feel comfortable with their accomplishments, it can be a challenge to motivate them to continue to learn, improve, and innovate. Nothing kills creativity faster than complacency—the sense that you've already gone the distance and can afford to rest on your laurels. That's when you and your team are at greatest risk, for while you are taking your eyes off the prize your competitors are not. Suddenly, you find that coasting is costing you market share as changes are being implemented by start-ups in the field. Or advances in AI have revolutionized areas of the business and you're coming too late to the game.

So how do you keep your team curious and on their toes when they feel they've already proven their worth? By making sure that everyone understands that change is a fact of life, and that applies more than ever to the life of every company. Again, a leader must orchestrate a balance between celebrating achievements and preventing the stagnation that sets in with complacency.

There are a number of specific behaviors that you or members of your team may exhibit, which are clear signs of complacency:

- People start giving the business's key performance indicators (KPIs) a cursory, superficial overview without doing an in-depth study of the details to learn more about what is going on. They are too quick to trust that everything is going fine.
- They stop paying attention, disregarding warning signs that may indicate a potential decline in sales or market share.
- They forget that competitors are improving daily. If your team isn't keeping up with changes and striving to break new ground, your company won't continue to lead.
- They stop listening and learning and tell themselves they've already won. That's a sure sign that they are no longer committed to the team but are splitting off on their own.
- They avoid conflicts and no longer challenge one another. You notice they've adopted the mindset *Why rock the boat if the business is doing*

well? Consequently, the business stops benefiting from different points of view. What helped the company become successful hits a roadblock and there's a dangerous slowdown in the learning curve.

- People seem to be less enthusiastic about the mission and are no longer curious about how to make changes to improve the business.

One way to fight against overconfidence and complacency is to remain humble and grounded even when you're riding high. That may be more difficult than it sounds because success is seductive. Our egos want to believe all the praise and to feel that we don't have anything more to prove, when the exact opposite is true. What we need to prove most is that we won't get carried away by our own sense of self-worth. That means constantly taking stock of what our primary purpose is and being alert to what is happening in the world around us so we can better serve our customers. If we put them ahead of ourselves, we have a better chance of keeping focused and staying grounded. We must remain attuned to the needs of our customers and our associates who are working tirelessly to give the best service possible in our brick-and-mortar stores and online. A leader has to be a role model for everyone in the art of being humble. And that means always listening and learning and keeping true to the goals that guided you early on.

A danger of complacency is that people cease to be as analytical as they need to be. They don't dive into the available data to see what information it can tell us about buying habits and patterns that could signal a change in trends. We must never forget that "retail is detail," and if we stop paying close attention to the numbers we are bound to make faulty business decisions and miss the early warning signs that something is off.

One of the ways we keep people from becoming complacent at the company is by holding "cultural meetings" where we bring in associates who have demonstrated Walmart's values to share their stories with the team. These serve as constant reminders to all of us not to coast or slack off, but to go the extra mile to serve our customers, respect them and each other, and continuously try to improve our own performance. I believe these meetings are crucial to keeping our company culture alive over so many decades. In every meeting you can feel the sense of enthusiasm people bring to their work—it's electric and energizes all of us.

At one meeting I interviewed an associate who was truly inspiring. We had heard about her from a member of our executive committee who had been doing a store visit and saw her get excited as she told a customer about our education memberships, which affordably help people in Mexico to obtain a high school equivalency certificate online in only five months. She said that she personally had purchased the membership because she never had the opportunity to attend high school and that now she was thrilled she was going to earn her certificate. For her, it was important to show her kids the importance of going to school. She was so persuasive in selling the membership because she was drawing on her own experience. When I spoke with her, you could feel everybody leaning into what she was saying. We were all learning from her example, seeing how she was using her own life story to help others achieve their goals. By appreciating and honoring the individuals who are reinforcing the company's values, we remind ourselves to practice them as well.

The Leader's Purpose

Gui

Leaders, like Walmart's founder, Sam Walton, are the architects who create the reason their companies exist. They build an organization to reflect their vision, purpose, and values, and make them the focus for future innovation.

I always tell people that I do not get paid to do well but to take the company to its maximum potential. Achieving our targets is not enough; we need to always strive to improve even when we've met our goals. The aim is to reach our maximum potential in all areas. And that potential is a moving target; even when you feel you know the direction you want to take, there are external factors impacting an organization's growth. The only fixed point is your purpose, the company's reason for being. That's the DNA of the company and will determine the behaviors of everyone on the team. Whenever we feel a little bit arrogant or complacent, we always have to go back to our DNA. In Walmart's case, that purpose is helping people live better.

That's ultimately what our transformation was all about. That's why I felt it was imperative to make it happen. The more we succeed, the more I see new opportunities that will benefit our customers and other stakeholders. But sometimes I ask myself, *How can I convince my team to do even more?* We're already doing well and everybody is very busy, so that can make me question how much I'm asking of them. I'm afraid to bring up new ideas. When I bring them to the table, my team either rejects them or looks at me in a way that makes me feel bad for pushing them to do more. There are times that my vision exceeds the reality of what they can do at a given point in time. A leader has to know when their team has reached their saturation point. What is the line between enough and too much? The temptation to ask them to do more is always there.

Creating the Capacity to Do More

Carlos

One of the main tasks of leadership is to focus the organization's resources on its chosen strategic priorities and to make sure the team has the operational capacity to deliver them. If you draw on resources that are already feeling overwhelmed, you will create conflict and not achieve the desired outcome. Sequencing is essential when convincing your team to do more for your customers. As we discussed in chapter 8, the leader is like a conductor who must determine the appropriate pace and rhythm of the team's performance. It's equally important to consider *when* you ask your team to take on more tasks as it is to consider *what* it is you're asking them to do. Aligning the ambition of your plan with the resources available requires careful calibration.

At Walmex, this was a good problem for them to have. How many businesses are excelling as they search for new ways to help people live better? Luckily, Gui's powers of persuasion ("the Gui Factor") combined with the organization's powerful sense of purpose to bring about changes that may have overtaxed another company. But it's a combination of the right leadership working in concert with the right purpose—having one or the other alone isn't enough to implement innovative transformation. Both parts of the equation are necessary.

Gui

A successful company creates benefits for all its stakeholders, starting with its associates in the field and its customers. The Walmex associates were the first to understand how our transformation aligned with our central purpose. They saw that our initiatives would expand our reach and help our customers on more fronts, which would enhance our business as well as expand career opportunities for them.

Our key suppliers were another group that quickly grasped how our transformational strategies could complement theirs. Many of them also had meaningful purposes that were driving their businesses, and there were substantial points of common interest that we shared, including an emphasis on affordable pricing, health care, and helping low-income customers. Working collaboratively allowed us to be more ambitious in our plans and more successful in delivering results. For example, food producers were keenly interested in helping us build our health membership; they saw the ways this could be linked to the kinds of food people would be encouraged to buy.

Our health memberships had wide-reaching impact, increasing the healthcare services available to our customers at a price they could afford. We gave our customers the incentive to buy into this program by offering them a 5% discount in our pharmacies when they became members. At first, this may have appeared to be a bad business decision as the discount was bigger than the cost of the membership. But there was a payoff that came in the form of increased customer loyalty to our pharmacies. As our customers improved their health, we improved our business, developing more new ideas and initiatives that would benefit those who signed up for our program.

By collaborating with our business partners, Walmex created the capacity to do more, making sure that we had the ability to translate our vision and goals into a sustainable reality.

Transformational Learning

Carlos

Throughout this book, Gui and I have charted the essential elements of the transformational learning process. Here, in brief, is a recap of the steps each leader must take when considering or planning a transformation:

- Start by questioning and challenging the organization's underlying assumptions and beliefs about the sustainability of its success.

Whatever brought you to the current level of achievement may not continue to be relevant in the future. What new ideas and innovations may be needed to move forward?

- Revitalize or discover the purpose that will give deeper meaning to why the organization does what it does, the compelling motive for its existence. If that purpose had been the North Star at one time, have you or your team lost sight of it or strayed too far afield from it?

- Engage the hearts and minds of the people of your organization by reinforcing that vital purpose. This can only be done if you've identified the universal humanity that's inherent in the mission.

- As a leader, you must define on a personal level why *your* life matters, what you stand for, and what you want your legacy to be. To paraphrase Nietzsche, The person who has a *why* to live for can bear almost any *how*. How can you advocate with passion on behalf of the company's purpose unless you also know what gives your own life meaning?

- Establish clear goals that are in alignment with the higher purpose. In doing so, you'll want to eliminate ambiguities and misunderstandings, so people commit to achieving the goals you've described.

- Set specific objectives and targets to be reached to provide benchmarks during each aspect of the transformation.

- Communicate a plan that consists of clear tactics and action steps, outlining the what, how, who, and when for each objective.

- Actively promote and practice learning on an ongoing basis. As the process advances, your new experiences and insights will lead to adjustments and adaptations that will improve the final results. As a leader, encourage your team to work cooperatively to learn and grow in order to make the transformation successful.

- Learn to tell a compelling story about what happened and how it was done.

The title of Dr. Marshall Goldsmith's best-selling book *What Got You Here Won't Get You There* speaks directly to the concept of continual learning as a means of self-growth and growing your company. We have also referred to Simon Sinek throughout our book, and there's a particular quote of his from

The Infinite Game that has been a touchstone for me and I hope will be useful to all leaders: "Infinite-minded leaders understand that 'best' is not a permanent state. Instead, they must strive to be 'better.' 'Better' suggests a journey of constant improvement and makes us feel like we are being invited to contribute our talents and energies to make progress in that journey."

Through the evolution and continuous learning of its leadership, Walmex achieved remarkable results. Two key factors were the power of its purpose and the outstanding ability of Gui and his colleagues to communicate that vision throughout the organization.

Rules for Staying in the Game

> "Every champion was once a contender that refused to give up."
> —Rocky Balboa

Carlos

In this book we aimed to provide readers with an inside look at how a leader can effectively change their leadership behavior to effect changes in the company.

Gui

I have found that if a leader is open to change—and if that mindset is evident to others—a company becomes more open to transforming itself too. I believe that my transformation facilitated the process of transformation in our organization and in many of our leaders as well.

Carlos

As you have read, what folks at Walmex coined as "the Gui Factor" became shorthand for Gui's leadership style, a combination of passion, high energy, purpose, and genuine curiosity about the world. I would ask every leader to look inside themselves and find those unique, special qualities, *their own factor*, that will motivate people to join them on even the most challenging of endeavors. And keep in mind that part of Gui's inspirational quality is his willingness and courage to be vulnerable, to admit mistakes, to apologize, and to commit to changing his own behavior, even when the stakes were at their highest and all eyes of the company were on him. That courage is a piece of "the Gui Factor" that I would encourage those in leadership positions to aspire to.

Gui

I'm filled with gratitude for the personal transformation I've undergone and the positive impact it has had on Walmex. Looking back, I regret that I didn't go through this process earlier in my life. However, I'm also aware that the reinvention I experienced required a certain level of maturity and resilience I didn't possess before.

I feel prepared to pursue my current goals and to grow in new ways as I pursue other ambitions in the future. I'm aware that there is always a possibility of failure, but I'm willing to take the risk and remain open to learning and changing. As Elbert Hubbard said, "The greatest mistake you can make in life is continually fearing that you'll make one."

Carlos

I'm impressed by Gui's openness regarding future possibilities. A leader with extensive experience who remains a confident yet humble learner is precisely what most ambitious companies are seeking in a CEO as they strive to stay relevant in the future.

Gui

The more you learn, the more you succeed. We all know that success is a key factor in retaining and attracting talent. The more you strive for success, the more open you must be to the intention of reinvention: receiving feedback, gaining knowledge, and using it to develop further. The learning loop never ends and is an essential part of an infinite endeavor.

Gui and Carlos

We wrote this book with the intention of showing readers how an organizational transformation was connected to a place deep within the leader. An aspiration to make something significant happen. Something meaningful that the heart yearns for while the brain deliberates how to execute it. To move into action from this ambivalent position takes courage, determination, and clarity of purpose because the possibility of failure and its potential consequences is lurking around the corner.

As we revisited the turbulent years of our transformation, we were able to reflect on paths not taken as well as decisions made that seemed daunting at the time but now feel like they were always part of the plan. The pattern of our lives seems to take on a certain inevitability only when viewed in retrospect. The fact is we were always discovering, always learning, and often improvising based on a desire to always improve. We still are.

The great novelist E. M. Forster once wrote, "Only connect." Perhaps that's the primary lesson of this book. The rest, as they say, is commentary. We hope *Reinventing the Leader* will help you learn to connect better to your customers, your team, and yourself. The journey of discovery is ongoing, and we see that fact as inspiring. The moment you believe you know everything is the moment you have already started to decline and to play a finite game. We believe the infinite game is not only more long-lasting but also more enjoyable.

Love what you do and remember that teams achieve more than individuals working on their own. As a leader, you can take people to places they would never get to alone. There is nothing better than seeing people succeed and knowing you played a role in helping them get there.

Life is short but we should not make it small. We encourage you to set ambitious goals, listen deeply, work as a team player, and play an infinite game. Most of all, have fun on your journey.

LEARNING POINTS FOR SUCCESSFUL LEADERS

Reinventing Yourself to Transform Your Company

Reinventing Yourself

- **Lesson:** Resolve to evolve.

  > "The smartest and most successful people I know
  > are the people who are constantly evolving,
  > always learning. It does not end with school."
  > —Stephanie Ruhle

  > "The most important thing in life is to stop saying
  > 'I wish' and start saying 'I will.' Consider nothing
  > impossible, then treat possibilities as probabilities."
  > —Charles Dickens

  > "Do not imagine that you will make people
  > friends by showing your superiority over them; it
  > is what they will neither admit nor forgive."
  > —William Hazlitt

Transform Your Company

Here, we're going to give Walmart founder Sam Walton the last word:

- **Lesson:** Work collectively to achieve a higher purpose. Give meaning to your mission and you will succeed.

  > "If we work together, we'll lower the cost of living for
  > everyone . . . we'll give the world an opportunity to
  > see what it's like to save and have a better life."
  > —Sam Walton

Appendix: A Library for Successful Leaders

The Content Trap: A Strategist's Guide to Digital Change by Bharat Anand

Loonshots: How to Nurture the Crazy Ideas That Win Wars, Cure Diseases, and Transform Industries by Safi Bahcall

Danger in the Comfort Zone: From Boardroom to Mailroom—How to Break the Entitlement Habit That's Killing American Business by Judith M. Bardwick

Transitions: Making Sense of Life's Changes by William Bridges, PhD, with Susan Bridges

Dare to Lead: Brave Work. Tough Conversations. Whole Hearts. by Brené Brown

Now, Discover Your Strengths by Marcus Buckingham & Donald O. Clifton, PhD / From Gallup

The Power of Myth by Joseph Campbell with Bill Moyers

El Muro Digital by Luiz Ferezin (Spanish edition)

Man's Search for Meaning by Viktor Frankl

True North: Leading Authentically in Today's Workplace, Emerging Leader Edition by Bill George and Zach Clayton

Conversational Intelligence: How Great Leaders Build Trust and Get Extraordinary Results by Judith E. Glaser

What Got You Here Won't Get You There by Marshall Goldsmith with Mark Reiter

Just Listen: Discover the Secret to Getting Through to Absolutely Anyone by Mark Goulston

Sapiens: A Brief History of Humankind by Yuval Noah Harari

Thrive: The Third Metric to Redefining Success and Creating a Life of Well-Being, Wisdom, and Wonder by Arianna Huffington

Exponential Organizations 2.0: The New Playbook for 10x Growth & Impact by Salim Ismail, Peter H. Diamandis, and Michael S. Malone

The New Leadership Literacies: Thriving in a Future of Extreme Disruption and Distributed Everything by Bob Johansen

Immunity to Change: How to Overcome It and Unlock the Potential in Yourself and Your Organization by Robert Kegan and Lisa Laskow Lahey

Leading Change by John P. Kotter

The Leadership Challenge: How to Make Extraordinary Things Happen in Organizations by James M. Kouzes and Barry Z. Posner

Learning Leadership: The Five Fundamentals of Becoming an Exemplary Leader by James M. Kouzes and Barry Z. Posner

The Advantage: Why Organizational Health Trumps Everything Else in Business by Patrick M. Lencioni

Digital @ Scale: The Playbook You Need to Transform Your Company by Jürgen Meffert and Anand Swaminathan

Hit Refresh: The Quest to Rediscover Microsoft's Soul and Imagine a Better Future for Everyone by Satya Nadella

The Digital Transformation Playbook: Rethink Your Business for the Digital Age by David L. Rogers

The Infinite Game by Simon Sinek

Scrum: The Art of Doing Twice the Work in Half the Time by Jeff Sutherland and J. J. Sutherland

Zen Mind, Beginner's Mind: Informal Talks on Zen Meditation and Practice by Shunryu Suzuki

Made in America: My Story by Sam Walton with John Huey

Acknowledgments

From Guilherme:

This book could not have been written without the help and support I have received from many people during my career.

I have learned from so many people that it is impossible to list all of them. But there are some people who have had a greater impact on my professional development:

Carlos Marin, my dear friend, partner, and coach.

Professor Moises Sznifer, who was a great mentor.

Humberto de Campos, who was responsible for sending me abroad and rescued me in a difficult moment of my career.

John Ripley, who taught me a lot and always gave me great advice.

Rudy Markham, a wise man who was key to my transition to senior management.

Pedro Padierna, a great mentor.

Vinicius Prianti, who taught me a lot about business, leadership, and trust.

Mark Chimsky, we could not have written this book without your help.

Dana Newman, our literary agent, for understanding our vision of this book from our first meeting and connecting us with the ideal publisher, Matt Holt Books.

My brother, Raul, who designed the book cover and has always inspired me.

To the entire team at Matt Holt Books, an imprint of BenBella Books, for trusting that we would deliver a book that would be meaningful and benefit readers. A particular debt of gratitude to Matt Holt, Katie Dickman, Ariel Fagiola, Mallory Hyde, Kerri Stebbins, and Brigid Pearson for helping us make this book a reality.

Walmart leaders Doug McMillon, David Cheesewright, Judith McKenna, Enrique Ostalé, and Eduardo Solarzano, who trusted me to run Walmart de Mexico and Central America and from whom I learned a lot. My reinvention would never have occurred without your support, advice, and trust.

To all my colleagues at Walmart. I have learned a lot from you and could never succeed without your support, contribution, and trust. Special recognition to Beatriz Núñez, Eduardo de la Garza, and Ale Paczka.

From Carlos:

First, I want to thank my dear friend and coauthor Guilherme "Gui" Loureiro. In the journey of writing this book, your trust, support, creativity, and camaraderie have been invaluable. From our many conversations to celebrating our small victories, your presence has made the endeavor richer. Thank you for sharing your wisdom, passion, and friendship.

I am grateful to my friend Dr. Marshall Goldsmith, a world-renowned business executive educator and coach. He has impacted countless individuals through his wisdom and generosity, and I am lucky to be one of them. Thank you, Marshall. "Life is good."

I deeply appreciate our esteemed editor Mark Chimsky for his professional dedication, invaluable guidance, insightful feedback, and steady encouragement. All of which made this book possible.

Our literary agent, Dana Newman, deserves recognition for finding the right home for our book. Thank you, Dana, for your capable assistance and advocacy.

My sincere gratitude to our publisher, Matt Holt. You made me feel like an old friend from the very beginning, by sharing that we had practically been neighbors a few years ago and discovering that we had several mutual good friends. Thank you, Matt, for believing in our work. My gratitude to your amazing team of professionals: Katie Dickman, Ariel Fagiola, Mallory Hyde, Kerri Stebbins, and Brigid Pearson.

And, of course, my special thanks to our talented Raul Loureiro, my coauthor's brother, for designing the book's cover.

I am grateful to my highly respected community of colleagues at The Learning Network. We have been meeting once a year since 1997 to learn from and support each other. Your wisdom and friendship have had an indelible impact on my journey. It has been an honor for me to be a part of such an extraordinary group of professional authorities in our fields of executive leadership and organizational development.

I would like to express my gratitude to all the executive clients from around the world who placed their trust in me to contribute to their professional development journeys. It has been an honor to have collaborated with you and your colleagues. Thank you very much for what I also learned from every one of you in the process.

About the Authors

Guilherme Loureiro

Guilherme Loureiro is a visionary leader who has gained renown for successfully leading the transformation of Walmex, the leading retailer in Mexico with 230,000 associates and a current market cap of $65 billion (USD). Seven years ago, Walmex (comprised of Walmart Mexico and Central America) was a brick-and-mortar retailer, and since then Gui and his team have built it into a digital company as well that is a key player in e-commerce, offering an ecosystem of digital products and services. While implementing this transformation, the company continued to grow both sales and profits at a fast pace. The share price has moved from 38 Mexican pesos when he started to 76 Mexican pesos today.

Recently, Gui was named Chairman of the Board for Walmex and Regional CEO for Canada, Chile, Central America, and Mexico, expanding his leadership responsibilities to include the company's large-scale retail presence in each country. He has a total of more than 14 years of experience as a CEO, with eight years as CEO of Walmex, the biggest Walmart operation outside of the United States, and two years as CEO for Walmart Brazil and four years as CEO of Unilever Mexico. He started his career as a management trainee in the finance area of Unilever Brazil. He spent 25 years working for Unilever and had multiple roles as Global Head of Strategy, Chairman of Unilever Ventures, Global Head of M&A, CEO Mexico, CFO Americas, and CFO Brazil.

Gui graduated in Business Administration from Fundação Getulio Vargas in São Paulo, Brazil, where he also earned a master's and a doctorate degree.

Among other courses, he attended The TGMP at Harvard Business School during 2002.

Gui is a noted speaker who has given talks about transformation at Microsoft Mexico, Honeywell Latin America, and Nestlé Mexico. He was a guest speaker at two IMD courses at Mondelēz, a United States company.

He is also a member of YPO, a prestigious community of more than 30,000 influential global leaders and change-makers.

Gui has also been interviewed by *CEO Magazine* and *McKinsey Quarterly*, which also featured his Walmex colleagues Beatriz Núñez and Cristian Barrientos, and was written by José Ricardo Cota, Thomas Kilroy, and Eduardo Malpica. In addition, he has been featured in cover stories in numerous Mexican magazines like *Líderes* and *Expansión*, and in the Brazilian publication *Exame*.

Carlos E. Marin

With 30 years of experience in the field of leadership development, Carlos Marin is a highly regarded executive leadership coach who has worked with many of the top 100 corporations in the world, with well-established results. He specializes in helping senior leaders and their teams in diverse cultural and international settings achieve measurable and sustained positive changes in their leadership behavior. As an executive coach, Carlos has led major organizational change initiatives in partnership with top leaders and executives.

Carlos's professional specialties involve executive team integration, authentic communication, transitions management, helping leaders become coaches and mentors, and designing and implementing large-scale organizational multi-rater (360-degree) feedback systems as well as complementary leadership development initiatives.

His clients include global businesses in the aerospace, banking and financial services, biotechnology, communications, consumer products, hospitality and entertainment, manufacturing, management consulting, pharmaceutical, technology, and utilities industries.

The companies that have used his executive leadership coaching services include American Express; Dell, Ernst & Young; Merck Sharp & Dohme; Coca-Cola; Hershey's; Lowes; Sempra Energy; Synthetic Genomics (now Viridos); and Wells Fargo.

Carlos's professional experience includes serving as the vice president of the Human Development Training Institute, a national training and publishing company based in San Diego, California, specializing in educational leadership skills training.

He was chancellor of National University, San Diego California International Campus in San José, Costa Rica, where he led fully USA-accredited master's in business administration degree programs with specialties in several international business disciplines. He has also been senior partner of The Washington Quality Group based in Madrid, Spain, a European pioneer consulting firm in the field of research-based executive coaching and business leadership development.

As a partner in the consulting firm Keilty Goldsmith and Co. in La Jolla, California, Carlos headed the firm's operations in Latin America.

Carlos has contributed to the book *Learning Journeys: Lessons in Becoming Great Mentors and Leaders*, later reissued under the title *Learn Like a Leader: Today's Top Leaders Share Their Learning Journeys*, edited by Marshall Goldsmith, Beverly Kaye, and Ken Shelton. In their starred review, *Publishers Weekly* calls *Learn Like a Leader* "a must-read for anyone interested in leadership, management, organizational design or personal development," and that "this inspiring collection of stories will enable individuals and groups to find deeper meaning in the work they do."

Carlos has a BS in Psychology from Michigan's University of Olivet and master's degrees in Educational Psychology and Guidance Counseling from Michigan State University, with advanced post-graduate studies at MSU in Leadership and Organizational Development.